EX AUDITU

An International Journal of Theological Interpretation of Scripture

Volume 10 1994

Ex Auditu is published annually by Pickwick Publications, 4137 Timberlane Drive, Allison Park, Pennsylvania 15101-2932, U.S.A.

Subscriptions
- Individuals:
  - U.S.A. - $15.00
  - Canada - $12.00 (in U.S. Funds)
  - All other countries - $15.00 (in U.S. Funds)
  - Students - $10.00
- Institutions:
  - U.S.A. - $25.00
  - Canada - $20.00 (in U.S. Funds)
  - All other countries - $25.00 (in U.S. Funds)

Indexed in *Religion Index One: Periodicals*, published by the American Theological Library Association, Chicago, Illinois, available online in the ATLA Religion Database through BRS Information Technologies (Latham, New York); DIALOGUE Information Services (Palo Alto, California); *Internationale Zeitschriftenshau für Bibelwissenschaft und Grenzgebeite; Religious and Theological Abstracts*; and *Old Testament Abstracts*.

Please address all subscription correspondence and change of address information to Pickwick Publications.

ISSN 08883-0053

EX AUDITU

An International Journal of Theological Interpretation of Scripture

THE EDITORIAL BOARD MEMBERS AND CONSULTANTS represent various disciplines and denominations. Theological Interpretation of Scripture is a task to be taken seriously by scholars who are committed to the Christian faith and tradition. However, as one editorial consultant stated: "let people gradually get used to the idea that a sane hermeneutics is both oriented in advance toward agreement/consent and is simultaneously exigent, discriminating, critical."

EDITORIAL CONSULTANTS

EX AUDITU

Volume 10 1994

CONTENTS

INTRODUCTION

No "institution" is so necessary, vulnerable, frustrating, or exalted as the church. The failures of the church both in history and in the present are notorious. Complaints against the church have become truisms. The church is too timid in confronting problems, too devoted to its own security, too hypocriticial to be believed, too irrelevant to be heeded, and too shallow in its thinking to lead and energize. Numerous people have been so scarred by churches that they have retreated from corporate faith to an individualistic relation to God. For all the complaints, for all the failures, the church still stands. The church still has a message and a task. People still come with the hope for healing and a place of service, and the church is continually being renewed to follow the leading of Jesus Christ. The potential for what the church could be still calls us to rethink and recommit our energies on behalf of the people of Christ.

Why do people keep coming to churches? Surely the reasons are straightforward. They come seeking authenticity, a sense of the presence of God, a sense of fit with other people a chance that someone might care or even love, the hope that insight will be provided for life, and a place to do something with their lives that is worthwhile.

The very definition of the church carries a built-in tension and inherent difficulties. On the one hand, the church is composed of those who have been separated to Christ. People are to be different from the society around them because of their allegiance to Christ. The church is a "holy" community. On the other hand, the church is a community for the care of fractured lives. People are to be accepted as they are into a loving, caring community. In addition, the church is always in the process of reformulation as it lives out faith in an ever-changing society. Many of the difficulties of being church arise along the borders between these dynamics. Are there boundaries to the church and does it have a fixed identity, or is it an "open" community? What does discipleship really mean?

The North Park Symposium for the Theological Interpretation of Scripture took place October 14-16, 1994, to discuss the church. The primary concern was the identity and the mission of the church. Such symposia can never treat all the relevant texts or aspects of the subject. Unfortunately, unexpected personal problems for one of the participants meant that a paper focused on Ephesians 2:11-22 and the problem of racism could not be included. This text is possibly the primary ecclesiological text in the NT. Let it be said in this introduction: racism has no place in the church of Jesus Christ. To state it more positively, the church has as part of its discipleship the rejection of all racist actions and ideas.

The introductory article by Don Miller was not presented at the symposium, but is provided as a general frame of reference for the other articles that are more limited in scope. Appreciation is expressed to all of the authors for their investment in the symposium and the journal. No suggestion is made that all participants were in agreement, and as always, the views expressed are those of the individual authors. But with the articles comes a challenge to rethink our corporate discipleship. By way of summary, these articles assert that the church is the necessary context within which we understand Jesus, rethink ethics, and define ourselves and our relation to society.

The original form of the article on 1 Samuel 2 by Stanley Walters was accompanied by detailed technical notes on the Hebrew text explaining the translation choices offered. The sermon from the worship service and an annotated bibliography are included.

The next symposium will take place October 13-15, 1995, at North Park Theological Seminary. The topic will be "Biblical Law and Liberty." For information, please write Ms. Jackson Blanchard, North Park Theological Seminary, 3225 W. Foster, Chicago, IL 60625.

Klyne Snodgrass
The Editor

An Announcement

North Park Theological Seminary in Chicago, Illinois is pleased to announce that the eleventh Symposium on Theological Interpretation of Scripture will take place October 13-15, 1995. The Symposium will start at 1:30 p.m. on October 13 in Nyvall Hall and will extend through noon on October 15.

The theme of the symposium will be Biblical Law and Liberty. The following persons have agreed to make presentations:

Dr. Erhard Gerstenberger	*Old Testament*
Dr. Kathryn Greene-McCreight	*Theology*
Dr. I. John Hesselink	*Theology*
Dr. Dean McBride	*Old Testament*
Dr. Carol Norén	*Sermon*
Dr. Richard Pierard	*History*
Dr. Ronald J. Ricci	*Law*
Dr. Charles H. Talbert	*New Testament*
Dr. Robert Taylor	*Law*
Dr. Frank Thielman	*New Testament*

Persons interested in attending the sessions should write before September 1, 1995 to:

Ms. Jackson Blanchard
North Park Theological Seminary
3225 W. Foster Avenue
Chicago, Illinois 60625

Meals may be taken at North Park, and assistance will be provided in finding nearby lodging.

A NEW TESTAMENT VIEW OF THE CHURCH AND ITS FAITH*

DONALD G. MILLER

THE NATURE OF THE CHURCH

The word "church" is a very flexible word. It means many things, and different things to different people. It may even mean several things to the same person. For example, one may say, "Let's go to church." To what is he or she going? Another says, "I grew up in the church." What does that mean? Still another may insist, "The church ought to do something about it." What is this church that the person thinks should act? "We go to Dr. So and-So's church," affirms someone else. Is it really Dr. So-and-So's church? "At my church," continues another, "we have a good youth program." In what sense can a church be my church? And is the church a place where programs are in order? It is often argued, "The church keeps up the moral tone of a community." Is that the business of the church? "The best people belong to the church," we are sometimes told. Is the church, then, the society of the socially and morally acceptable?

These various expressions show how vague and uncertain is our idea of the church. It is strange that we can say so many different things about the same word. It is well, therefore, to face the question of what the church really is.

Popular Conceptions of the Church

Our search for an answer to this question may well be prefaced by a look at some of the popular ideas people have of the church. To some the church is a building. On a plot of ground at the corner of a farm, or on a village square, or on the busy street of a bustling city, or nestling in a narrow ravine made by a row of skyscrapers in a modern metropolis, there stands a building—and to many, that building is the church. We can point to it, as we do the store, or the bank, or the theater, and say, "There is the church." Even one who never darkens the door of that building may be heard to say, "I pass the church every day on my way to work."

Others, aware that even a bank, or a store, or a theater is far more than a building—for a bank without financial transactions is not a bank, nor a store without goods a

*This is an edited version of materials from the author's book, now out of print, *The Nature and Mission of the Church.* Richmond, Virginia: John Knox Press, 1957.

store, nor a theater without actors or film a theater—see that the church is not merely the building which goes by that name, but in some way exists in the people and the activities which go on in the building. To them, the church is like a club, or a lodge, or a fraternity. It is a group of like-minded people who enjoy each other's company. By their own choice they have banded together in a human organization for mutual benefit or enjoyment. They give money to keep the building in repair, to heat it in winter and to cool it in summer, and to support the various activities in which they engage. This provides a stimulus to the native religious side of their nature and offers them a channel for social fellowship with a high type of people.

Some who are more outgoing in their desire to help other people think of the church as an effective social agency. It exists basically to serve the needs of the poor, or the unfortunate, or the uneducated. It is a society where social passion is to be kindled and maintained by religion. Its goal is humanitarianism. But since people are notoriously unlikely to be humane to others without the gracious influences of religion, the church exists to provide the religious energies which will conquer humanity's cruelty and quicken its kindness. The church might well be thought of as the religious arm of the community chest, or a Society for the Prevention of Cruelty to Human Beings.

Another view of the church is that it consists of an audience which comes weekly to listen to a great orator. A person gifted in speech and dynamic in personality, with perhaps a flair for the dramatic and the ability to produce emotion, gathers a group of followers who so love to hear him or her speak that they would not miss the opportunity for anything. This is what leads people to speak of "Dr. So-and-So's church." To them, that particular church is made up of this remarkable pulpiteer and the loyal group of people who come to hear or who feel that they get great good from the sermons. It is this also which frequently causes congregations to dwindle and wither away a few short months after such a person leaves a community for another one.

Several other ideas of the church may be added to these. Sometimes the church is thought of as a place where people come to get their problems solved—a sort of religious clinic. Again, the church is often understood to be a society for moral culture, a type of religious gymnasium where moral and spiritual exercises are designed to maintain or increase the moral health of individuals. Or, once more, many think of the church as the historic extension of some great past event. It is a society whose purpose is to perpetuate the memory of Jesus or the beginning of the Christian group, much as the D.A.R. rekindles the memory of the American Revolution, or the Huguenot Society the beginnings of the Huguenot movement.

The plain fact with which the New Testament confronts us is that no one of these, nor all of them together, is adequate. All of them may be phases, or accompaniments, of the church's life, but none of them is the church. To confuse the church with them would be like saying that a fire company consists in a group of people sitting in a fire station playing cards, or that a stock exchange is a place where people huddle in groups and shout to each other amidst the endless flow of ticker tape.

What, then, is the church? We shall seek first to discover from the New Testament what the nature, or essence, of the church is, then to draw from this certain qualities or characteristics which necessarily follow.

The New Testament Conception of the Church

The English word "church" comes from the Greek word *kyriakon*, which means "that which belongs to the Lord." This word is used only twice in the NT, once to designate the Lord's Supper (1 Cor 11:20), and once in speaking of the Lord's day (Rev 1:10). But "church" is especially used to translate another NT word which is closely related to the idea of "that which belongs to the Lord"—it is the word *ecclesia,* from which our word "ecclesiastical" comes, which describes the "*people* who belong to the Lord." This word is one of the favorite words of the NT, being used some 115 times. But the idea it embodies appears far more frequently than that. The NT writers are often speaking about "the people who belong to the Lord" when they do not use the word *ecclesia.*

The basic meaning of this word was merely a gathering of citizens summoned, or "called out," by a herald to meet in a public place for some special purpose. It later came to be used loosely for any public assembly of people for any reason. The NT, however, gives to this word a very special meaning. It uses it not merely to describe an assembly of people, but quite consistently speaks of *the* assembly or the church (Acts 8:1). This special use of the word has no parallel in secular Greek writings outside the NT. The only parallel comes from the Greek translation of the OT. There the expression "the *ecclesia* of God" or "the *ecclesia* of the Lord" is frequently found (e.g. Deut 31:30; 1 Kings 8:14). Obviously, therefore, when the NT writers use this expression found nowhere outside the OT, they must have been using it in its OT meaning. They were saying that "the church" is what the OT described as those who were "called out" of the world to be "the people who belonged to God" in a very special way. This connection of the church with the OT people of God is made unmistakably clear when Paul calls the church "the Israel of God" (Gal 6:16).

But when the church was formed, there was another Israel—the old Israel, the ancient people of God in whose veins flowed the blood of Abraham. What made the difference between this "old Israel" and the "new Israel"? The decisive thing was their attitude toward Jesus Christ. The old Israel had rejected Jesus as Messiah and had him condemned to death. The new Israel was made up of those who accepted Jesus as Messiah, and believed that he had been raised from the dead. They felt that the old Israel had forfeited the right to be the special "people who belonged to God" and that the Christian Church was now the true "people of God."

But they had become the "people of God" not because of anything they had done. They were such purely because of what Jesus had done. He had called them to himself as their Messiah. They had responded to his call. They had followed him when he was here in the flesh. They now believed that though he had been slain he was alive forevermore. They had been made "God's people" solely by the call, the life, the death, and the resurrection of Jesus. To be "the people of God," then, was identical with being "the people of Jesus." Paul could write to the Corinthian Christians that they were "the church of God" because they were "sanctified in Christ Jesus" and called "on the name of our Lord Jesus Christ" (1 Cor 1:2). Again, Paul referred to the Christians at Ephesus as "the church of the Lord which he obtained with his own blood" (Acts 20:28). Here it is plain that the Christian church was brought into being by Jesus, and that he had done it by his death—which, to Paul, always included the resurrection as the outcome of his death. The church, therefore, is the community of those who live by the power of the death and resurrection of Jesus.

This leads naturally to the two favorite terms used in the NT to describe the church; namely, the *temple of the Holy Spirit* and the *body of Christ.* As we shall see, these two expressions are very closely interrelated and are practically synonymous.

The church as God's temple and as Christ's body is to be understood in the light of its relation to Jesus Christ. *He* is God's temple. The church is *his* body. Apart from Him, neither temple nor body could have any meaning for the church. Let us see, then, how this is set forth in the NT.

In the OT the temple—and the tabernacle before it—was the place where God had chosen to dwell in the midst of his people. It was there that God met His people and they met him. It was there that God's glory was to be seen. It was there that God was worshiped. It was there that priests made sacrifices for sin. It was there that people came to learn God's law and to understand his will. It was there that children were dedicated to God and adults offered themselves to God as his servants. The temple was the place where every relation between a holy God and sinful humanity was to be established and maintained.

But the old temple had failed to achieve the ends for which it had been built. It had been desecrated and defiled and was worthy only of being destroyed. Once, in 587 B.C., it had been destroyed. Later it was rebuilt, but the failure of the earlier temple was repeated. Instead of being the place where God met humanity, it had become an impediment in the way of their meeting. Jesus, therefore, in decisive and dramatic action, entered the temple in judgment, indicating that it was no longer fulfilling its purpose. Instead of being "a house of prayer" it had become "a den of robbers" (Matt 21:13). Jesus also had to pronounce over the temple the sad words of doom: "There will not be left here one stone upon another, that will not be thrown down" (Matt 24:2).

But was the purpose for which the old temple stood never to be fulfilled? Yes, it would be fulfilled. The old temple was to be replaced by another and a better one. And that temple was the body of Jesus. From henceforth, God would meet humanity in him! That Jesus thus conceived of himself is quite plain in the gospel story. When he was on trial, one of the witnesses against him made the charge: "This fellow said, 'I am able to destroy the temple of God, and to build it in three days' " (Matt 26:61). A charge like this taken literally would have been absurd. It is obvious that it was misunderstood by the one who made it. But the charge shows that Jesus had said something about destroying a temple.

The Fourth Gospel makes plain what Jesus had meant by what he said. In John's account of the cleansing of the temple, when Jesus was asked for a sign of his authority to do it, he replied, "Destroy this temple, and in three days I will raise it up" (John 2:19). The Jews misunderstood him, thinking that he was talking about the temple of stone which stood before them. But the writer adds, "he spoke of the temple of his body," and then relates the saying to the death and resurrection of Jesus (John 2:21-22). In this way, Jesus was claiming that the true temple of God was no longer the structure of stone which stood before them. It was rather his own body, which his enemies were planning to put to death, but which would be raised to new life on the third day. Add to this the statement in John 1:14 that "the Word became flesh and dwelt [tabernacled] among us," and it is plain that Jesus' "flesh," his "body," was the new temple of God which was to take the place of the old temple.

The old temple would be destroyed never to rise again. On the other hand, the temple of Jesus' body would be destroyed in death, but would rise again at the resurrection. From now on, God would meet his people in Jesus. It was in him that God's "glory" was to be seen. In him God was to be worshiped. He was the great High Priest who made the sacrifice of himself for humanity's sin. In him men would learn God's law and understand his will. To him children would be dedicated, and people would offer themselves to God as his servants. In Jesus, every relation between a holy God and sinful humanity was to be established and maintained. Hence, when he died on the cross, the curtain of the old temple was torn in two (Matt 27:51), showing that the way into God's presence was no longer through the old sanctuary, but rather through the sanctuary of the risen body of Jesus. The true temple of God is the risen Lord!

But where does the church stand in relation to all this? Repeatedly, the church is called "God's temple" or "house" (1 Cor 3:16; Eph 2:21; 1 Tim 3:15; Heb 10:21; Rev 3:12.) It is also called "the body of Christ" (Rom 12:5; 1 Cor 12:27; Eph 1:23; 4:12; 5:30; Col 1:18, 24). If the true temple of God is the body of Jesus, how can the church be God's temple? The answer to this is to be found at Pentecost. There, after Jesus had died, risen, and ascended to the right hand of God, he returned in his Spirit to live in the church. He is still the temple of God, but he is living in his church. So, by virtue of his living presence in his church, it becomes the temple of God. And that temple which was Christ's body when he was on earth is now to be found in the church, which is his body on earth since the resurrection. God now tabernacles among humans in Jesus, as Jesus lives in His church.

The church, then, is made up of all those to whom the risen Christ has given his Spirit. It is the fellowship of those who believe in the resurrection, and to whom the living Christ is real. Where Jesus is, there is the church. And Jesus has promised that "where two or three are gathered in my name, there am I in the midst of them" (Matt 18:20). The church is the new people of God, made possible by the death and resurrection of Jesus, and created by his Spirit living in their midst. That is why Peter could say of the church, "You are a chosen race, a royal priesthood, a holy nation, God's own people . . . Once you were no people but now you are God's people" (1 Pet 2:9-10). The church is the community of the resurrection, the fellowship of people in whom God's Spirit dwells, the fraternity of the forgiven, the people who are called out of the world to belong to God, in order that their corporate life may consist in his worship and service.

Characteristics of the Church

If this be the church, then certain characteristics follow "as the night the day." They may here be traced only in bold lines.

The church is divine, not human. We do not make the church by our efforts; we receive it as a gift from God. The church is not created by a group of religious people banding together to form it. It was created by God through the resurrection of Jesus Christ. His resurrection ushered in the "new age" which shall abide when "this present age" is gone, when time shall be no more, and God shall be all and in all. This new life, "eternal life," is open to all who will receive it by faith. Those who are willing to identify themselves with Jesus Christ in his death and resurrection are already living in the sphere of his resurrection power. This no human achieves. It is the gift of God. Better organization, increased human effort, modernization of methods—all good in themselves—do not build the church. They are mere means by which the church expresses itself. Our primary task is to examine whether we are the church or not.

The church is a fellowship of faith, not an institution. The church does not consist of buildings or programs, but of people. Nor is the church made up of unbroken historic institutional forms, but of believers in the gospel. One is, therefore, not saved by outward adherence to an institution, but by faith in Christ. No one structural form of institutional life, nor any specific form of worship, is of the *essence* of the church. The church may express itself in history in many forms. Nor is the church made up of a hierarchy of clergy who dispense grace to laypeople. Various functions are given to various members of the church, just as different members of the body have various functions to perform. But no one of the members, nor any group of members, is the church. The church is the total body of believers, clergy and laity alike, who are "in Christ" and who together make up his body here on earth. The church is not a rigid structure, but a fellowship of all those in whose corporate life the Spirit of Christ dwells.

The church is corporate, not individualistic. (The Latin *corpus*, meaning "body" or the uniting of many members into one whole, gives us the English word "corporate" which best describes the "E Pluribus Unum" which is the church.) Just as a body is not made by collecting a hand here, and an arm there, and a foot somewhere else, and then putting them together, so the church is not made up of a group of isolated individuals who decide to unite for their common religious welfare. Furthermore, just as a hand has no possible existence apart from the body of which it is a part, neither does an individual Christian have any existence apart from the total church, the body of Christ. The church is not "a bouquet of believers," a collection of individual Christians brought together by mutual agreement. The church is an organism from which each member draws life. Christ is the church. And to be in him is to be in the church.

Our faith is personal, but not individual. It is the personal ingrafting into a corporate reality. When a nation surrenders in war, it is not a matter of each individual making a surrender. The corporate nation acts. The individual may go on fighting, without even knowing that the nation has surrendered. On hearing of the surrender, the individual must personally identify with the action of the corporate nation, but cannot act as an individual. The individual can act only as a part of the nation. So, when Christ triumphed over evil through his death and resurrection, he won a total corporate victory for humanity. We must personally appropriate this by faith, thus making his victory our victory. But it is not an individual action. It is the personal acceptance of an act done quite outside one's individual experience, and done for the whole race. Never is one less of an individual than when exercising personal faith in Christ. By that very act of faith, the individual is identified with Christ and with all others who are believers in Christ. That individual has moved from corporate involvement with sin and death into a corporate involvement with redemption and life. As P. T. Forsyth has said, the "same act which sets us in Christ sets us also in the society of Christ." To be in Christ, then, is to be in his body, the church. We may neglect our relation to Christ's people, but as long as we are in him we cannot destroy it. As the member of the surrendered nation is involved in the whole nation's action, so the believer is involved in the whole church. To join a church does not put us in the church. It merely publicly witnesses to what is already a fact.

The church is universal, not local. The church is not merely the particular congregation to which I belong, nor the denomination to which it adheres. When one unites with the church in any particular place, one unites with the church universal. The universal church is not made up by adding all local congregations together. A university is more than the sum total of the colleges which make it up. And, in one sense, the whole university is present in each of its colleges. So, rightly understood, the whole church is present in any local congregation. It is the whole people of God looking out on the world at that point. The word *ecclesia* in the NT is used to speak of the entire church, or of a local church, or even of a small group of Christians within a local church. The same word covers all cases. "The part is equal to the whole, because each part possesses, not a fragment of the Christ, but the whole Christ." Where people meet in Jesus' name, there he is—not just a part of him. The whole church is in him, and he is in the whole church.

If it were not for the barriers of time and space, when the church meets for worship all believers, from Adam to the end of time, would be present. But although time and space make that impossible physically, it is nonetheless true spiritually. The writer of Ephesians tells us that God's purpose was "to unite all things in Christ, things in heaven and things on earth" (See Eph 1:10). When any part of the church meets, then, it is in fellowship with every other part, including those already dead and those yet to be born.

The writer of Hebrews tells us that we are now in fellowship with "the assembly of the first-born who are enrolled in heaven . . . and . . . the spirits of just men made perfect" (Heb 12:23). To belong to the church, then, is to belong to all others who were, or now are, or ever shall be in the church. A local gathering of Christians is Christ, the whole Christ, present and making himself known there at that point. Paul said, "We who are many are one body" (1 Cor 10:17; see also Rom 12:5 and 1 Cor 12:12-27). The local church, therefore, is not a church; it is the church at that place. The church is one.

The church is the body of the living Christ, not the perpetuator of his memory nor the guardian of a tradition. From what has been said above, it is plain that the church has no existence unless the Spirit of the Living Christ lives in her now. The church does not exist to perpetuate the "spirit" of a great man long since dead, as a Browning Society seeks to keep alive the work of the great poet. In that case it would be the body of Christ mummified, like the body of Lenin—mute witness to the life of one who was alive but is now dead, save as his memory and work are perpetuated. But the church is no mummy, no mere lingering memorial to the past. Christ lives now and lives in the church. The church is the living vehicle of the living Lord who is very much alive now and rules the world from his position at the right hand of God. It is only as he lives now in the church, that the church is the church.

As the temple of God and the body of Christ, *the church exists not for her own sake, but solely for the glory of God.* The church is a worshiping community, whose worship is designed not for what we may get out of it, but that we may return to God the love we owe. This worship is rendered to God in the outgoing of our hearts to him in gratitude through prayer and praise. But worship consists also in service. True praise to God involves the surrender of all one is and has, to be used as an instrument in his hands for accomplishing what he wants done in the world. True worship involves "devoting the will to the purpose of God."

Consequently, the outlook of the church is not toward her self-preservation but toward the salvation of the world. As Christ had to die in order to save the world, so in her own measure the church has to die to be the instrument of that salvation. The central aim of the church, therefore, is not that of human societies, which are various forms of "co-operative egoism," or the pooling of "social self-interest." In so far as the church exists merely for the sake of serving its own members, or meeting the needs of a select few who have banded together for mutual betterment, it ceases to be the church. The church is an army, committed to the sacrifice of self, engaged in costly action in God's warfare against evil, looking forward to that day when "The kingdom of the world has become the kingdom of our Lord and of his Christ, and he shall reign for ever and ever" (Rev 11: 15).

THE FAITH OF THE CHURCH

The church survives by what it believes. It is a fellowship of faith, and by that faith it lives. We have seen that the church is not a sociological fact to be accounted for on any human terms. It is not a human association of like-minded people banded together for self-improvement or social betterment. It is rather a divine fellowship whose life is drawn from Christ. The church lives only because Jesus lives, and because his life flows into it and through it. It is kept alive, therefore, by what it believes about Jesus. It is sustained by all that is involved in its basic confession: Jesus Christ is Lord. Let us examine what the implications of his Lordship are for the faith of the church.

The Exclusiveness of Jesus' Lordship

If Jesus is Lord, he can brook no rivals. The very name "Lord" implies that he is "ruler," "one who has authority." Therefore, all others are his subjects. But this thought in the NT goes much beyond the mere meaning of the title itself. The early Christians poured unique content into the title "Lord" when they used it of Jesus. The meaning of this title for the Christians must be drawn from the OT. The very heart of the OT faith was this: "Hear, O Israel: The Lord our God is one Lord" (Deut 6:4). The basis on which the faith of Israel rested was that *there is but one God, and that God is absolute ruler of the universe*. People and nations, the forces of nature, and whatever spiritual powers there may be in the universe around us—all are ruled by him and subject to his authority. Since there is but one Lord, he is Lord of *all*. The nations are his "heritage," the ends of the earth are his "possession" (Ps 2:8).

Now the amazing thing about the early Christians is that they transferred to Jesus all that as Jews they had believed about God. Paul, for example, quotes an OT passage which speaks of God and dares to apply it to Jesus. Referring to Joel 2:32, he writes: "Every one who calls upon the name of the Lord will be saved" (Rom 10:13). But how is one saved? Paul adds: "If you confess . . . that Jesus is Lord . . . you will be saved" (Rom 10:9). Calling upon Jesus as Lord was the same thing as calling upon God as Lord. It is obvious, therefore, that all that Paul expected from God he expected from Jesus. The Lordship of Jesus over the world was as absolute as the Lordship of God.

If this be true, certain implications inescapably follow. For one thing, Jesus demands from people not admiration, sympathy, interest, approval; he demands surrender. To be a Christian is first of all to "bow the knee" to Jesus, to "crown Him Lord of all." Friend he was to the early Christians, as well as Counselor, Example, Guide. But before all this he was absolute Lord. "For the Lord our God the Almighty reigns" was the theme song of the early church (Rev 19:6).

It has been pointed out that in this sense Christianity is not a democracy but a monarchy. And it is not a constitutional monarchy, wherein subject and ruler agree on the limits of the rule. It is an absolute monarchy. People are subject to him not by a compact they have made with him, but because they belong to him. His Lordship, of course, is limited by his righteousness and his holy love. It is not arbitrary, for it is exercised as an expression of his gracious nature. But that gracious nature is not of our choice, and his kindness is not the result of an agreement which we have forced on him. It is the free exercise of his own nature. We are the beneficiaries of this, but are in no sense responsible for it. He reigns over us absolutely by virtue of his Lordship. It is our source of blessing that his Lordship is gracious. The church confronts the world, then, not primarily with an offer to heal its ills or solve its problems. Its first appeal is to rebels who have taken up arms against their Creator, an appeal which is nothing less than the demand for surrender. The gospel "faces the world with terms, and does not simply suffuse it with a glow," said P. T. Forsyth.

Another implication of Christ's absolute Lordship is that there is no other way of salvation for humans than surrender to Jesus. In this sense, Christianity is absolutely intolerant. Both Testaments are clear at this point. "For I am God, and there is no other," cries the prophet (Isa 45:22). What then? The conclusion is inevitable. "Turn to me and be saved, all the ends of the earth!" (Isa 45:22). If there is no God but one, then he is the God of all people, and there can be salvation in no other. The NT echoes this same uncompromising truth, save that it sees that the salvation of the one God is now made known in Jesus. Speaking of Jesus, Peter said in his second sermon recorded in the book of the Acts,

"And there is salvation in no one else, for there is no other name under heaven given among men by which we must be saved" (Acts 4: 12) .

This absoluteness of the Christian faith has long been a stumbling block to many. This is the "scandal" of our faith. How can the narrow stream of holy history recorded in the Bible, the history of a comparatively obscure and insignificant people, a history which to the secular historian is quite unimportant—how, it is asked, can this story have final meaning for the world? How can the salvation of all people in all ages rest on the death of an obscure peasant in a remote corner of the earth nearly two thousand years ago? This is the "offense" of the Christian faith. But offensive or not, *it is the faith of the church!*

Christ does not merely add something to the sum total of the world's knowledge. He is not merely the crown of an evolving process of enlightenment. He is not just the capstone to be placed upon the pillar of other religious faiths. Christ does not supplement other religions, he supplants them. This is not to say, of course, that there is no value in other religions, nor that the church is to despise or treat with contempt the best insights which others have discovered. In the sense of graciousness toward members of other faiths, Christianity by its nature is the most tolerant of all religions. It brings itself under the judgment of its Lord along with others and lives in penitence for its own failure fully to own Christ's Lordship. When it is true to itself, it never coerces. It never seeks to propagate itself by means other than those of moral suasion. It survives by its witness to the truth and by its moral power. As a theological student has recently written, Christianity approaches other religions "not with a faith that confuses politics with its message, nor with a faith that finds its strength in logical argumentation 'proving' its superiority to [them], but with the joy, the purity, and the redemption that the gospel of the resurrection holds out to all people."

Should the church grow proud and haughty, should self-will creep into its proclamation, it would thereby make an idol of itself, and thus deny the Lordship of Christ in its own life. But as to its message, it is absolutely intolerant and adamant. It claims the whole world for its Lord. It proclaims that all other efforts at salvation are vain. It does not pronounce on the fate of those who have never known Christ. It leaves them to the mercy of a gracious God in whose love their destiny lies. But it does insist without apology that if such are saved at last, it will be by Christ.

But why should this be considered blameworthy? If God has done a unique thing in Jesus Christ for all people, without which they are left in hopelessness and despair, is it the mark of pride and unworthy intolerance to tell them of this? If one should be caught in a crowded burning building with many doors, only one of which would open, would he be considered a bigot to proclaim to the desperate people with all the force at his command which door would open to their touch and lead them to safety? On the contrary, if he should hold his silence he would be blameworthy! Thus it is with the Christian proclamation. If Christians were proclaiming themselves, or proudly insisting that something which they had devised was superior to all other religious devices, this would be despicable. But the church does not proclaim itself, nor any way of life it has discovered, nor any achievement of its own which it feels is superior to that of others. The church proclaims that God, who by virtue of his creation is Lord of all people, has come to people in Jesus not only to show them that, though they are rebels, he still loves them, but also to offer them the way of escape from the human dilemma, to lift the mark of death on all things human. Is the church selfish to proclaim this? On the other hand, would it not be the supreme selfishness to fail to shout it from the housetops?

The Inclusiveness of Jesus' Lordship

If Jesus' Lordship is exclusive in that it supplants all other lordships, it is inclusive in that it covers the whole of life. It is the church's faith that Jesus is Lord of every aspect of human existence. To the Christian, religion is not a part of life—it is life. The whole of life is transformed by Christ. The "mind" is to be renewed by Christ (Rom 12:2). The will is to be subdued and relieved of its folly by "understand[ing] what the will of the Lord is" (Eph 5:17). The feelings, too, are to be cleansed. "I beseech you . . . to abstain from the passions of the flesh that wage war against your soul . . . so as to live for the rest of the time in the flesh no longer by human passions but by the will of God" (1 Pet 2:11; 4:2). Every element of individual behavior is to be brought under the white light of God's will and purpose. "And whatever you do, in word or deed, do everything in the name of the Lord Jesus" (Col 3:17).

But the corporate life of society is also to be brought under the Lordship of Jesus. His will is to prevail in every social relationship of life. Strong though natural family ties are, Jesus sets people into a larger family, the "household of faith," "the household of God" (Gal 6:10; Eph 2:19), the family over which he is Lord. Since his Lordship is absolute, the demands of human family kinship must be denied when they conflict with loyalty to him. "If any one," said Jesus, "comes to me and does not hate his own father and mother and wife and children and brothers and sisters, yes, and even his own life, he cannot be my disciple" (Luke 14:26). Obviously the word "hate" here on the lips of Jesus is not to be taken literally, but is an Oriental form of speech indicating the renunciation of anything which would conflict with the claims of God.)

Furthermore, strong though the bonds are which tie people to their nation, loyalty to Christ must take precedence over patriotism. For "our commonwealth is in heaven" (Phil 3:20). Although we are of necessity members of one nation or another, yet in reality we can never be content with any citizenship on earth. Life for us is "the time of our exile" (See 1 Pet 1:17). Christians are "strangers and exiles on the earth . . . seeking a homeland" (Heb 11:13-14). Final sovereignty, therefore, can never be given to any earthly government. Christ is "the ruler of kings on earth" (Rev 1:5), and loyalty to him must take precedence over the claims of any earthly authority. One of the most difficult problems the church faces in every generation is how to relate the limited allegiance it owes to earthly states to the absolute allegiance which belongs to Christ. But throughout the generations, when these two loyalties have clashed, the church has again and again proclaimed with its blood the Lordship of Christ over all of life.

All other aspects of society's life must likewise be brought into subjection to Christ, insofar as it is possible in a sinful situation. The claims of race must yield to his Lordship. The fact that one is a member of a particular race is less important to the Christian than that he is a member of the body of Christ. The artificial distinctions between people created by such things as wealth, social position, sex, educational privilege, possession of power through position, must be mastered by him who "emptied himself, taking the form of a servant" (Phil 2:7). To accept Christ's Lordship is to renounce all other lordships. All status which accrues from any attachments other than to him must be sacrificed. This could not have been put in clearer terms than those used by Jesus: "Whoever of you does not renounce all that he has [not only things, but status, earthly securities, and desires] cannot be my disciple" (Luke 14:33). If Christ is Lord, and the only Lord, and Lord of all, then the fundamental oneness of those who accept his Lordship transcends all the superficial distinctions among people. These are all made subservient to him who "is our peace, who has made us both one, and has broken down the dividing wall of hostility . . . that he might create in himself one new man . . . and might reconcile us both to God in one body through the cross, thereby bringing the hostility to an end" (Eph 2:14-16).

The Reality of Jesus' Lordship

Jesus' Lordship lies in the realm of fact, not of theory. It is a matter of history, not of idea. For one to be Lord does not mean for him to discuss or confer about the idea of lordship and to persuade people in their minds that his rule is a good thing. It is rather to meet people with terms to be accepted, which if not accepted must be established by action. Lordship is an achievement, not an idea. It is a reality, not a thought.

Few aspects of the Christian faith are more misunderstood by both its adherents and its enemies than this. Christianity is not a way of looking at life—a philosophy. It is not a way of living—an ethic. It is not a set of ideas about God—a theology. It involves all these but it is basically other than these. It is an *event, a deed, an accomplishment, a victory.* Speaking of his own work, Jesus said, "No one can enter a strong man's house and plunder his goods, unless he first binds the strong man; then indeed he may plunder his house" (Mark 3:27). In order to establish his Lordship, therefore, it was necessary that "the ruler of this world be cast out" (John 12:31). And that was not done by conference. It was done by costly action on a cross. The gospel is the "good news" that *God has acted on behalf of humans, to deliver them from the power of sin and death.* By this action, humans are set in a new relation to God, to themselves, and to each other. Instead of being an enemy of God, one becomes "reconciled to God by the death of his Son" (Rom 5:10) and "has passed from death to life" (John 5:24; 1 John 3:14). "Fellowship with one another" expressed in "love . . . in deed and in truth" is the relationship to other people (1 John 1:7; 3:18). These are not mere ideas. There are things which happen and are made true only by happening.

It is clear that the belief that God had done something in Christ "for us and for our salvation" was the heart of the faith of the early church. In spite of all differences of viewpoint and approach, all the NT leaders were in agreement concerning the central facts of their faith. This may be seen in the statement of Paul in 1 Cor 15:3ff.: "For I delivered to you as of first importance what I also received, that Christ died for our sins in accordance with the scriptures, that he was buried, that he was raised on the third day in accordance with the scriptures, and that he appeared to Cephas, then to the twelve. Then he appeared to more . . ." A few verses later he speaks of the fact that Christ's resurrection was "the first fruits" of a resurrection in which all "who belong to Christ" are to participate "at his coming" (1 Cor 15:23).

Here is the heart of the Christian faith. Paul insists that this was in no way an individual summary, a "slant" of his own. This he had "received" from the other apostles. He held this in common with them all. "Whether then it was I or they, so we preach and so you believed" (I Cor 15:11). And what was it that they held in common? It was that the gospel was the proclamation of a series of events wrought by God in Jesus Christ in behalf of humanity. Although Paul does not say it here, he implies what he says elsewhere, that Jesus was born as a "descend[ant] from David according to the flesh" (See Rom 1:3). His coming into the world "in accordance with the scriptures" (1 Cor 15:3) meant that the prophecies of the OT were fulfilled in him, and that the new age toward which the prophets were pointing had been inaugurated. This one who brought the new age did it by dying for our sins, by rising on the third day, and by ascending to the right hand of God, where he now reigns in exaltation "far above all rule and authority and power and dominion, and above every name that is named not only in this age but also in that which is to come" (Eph 1:20-21). But there is one other element in the proclamation—he will come again to "bring to light the things now hidden in darkness" and to "disclose the purposes of the heart" (1 Cor 4:5). This summary represents the central affirmation of the early church, the "good news" which they all believed, which had brought the church into being and by which its life was nurtured. And it all involves the simple affirmation that *something wonderful has happened!* It is neither theology, philosophy, nor ethics. It is a simple story of facts. Christ is Lord because these facts are true.

The presentation of these facts, however, always demands a response on the part of the hearer. If God has done something for us, we must accept it. Hence, the proclamation of the "good news" always ended in an appeal for decision. "Repent," was Peter's call at Pentecost, "and be baptized every one of you in the name of Jesus Christ for the forgiveness of your sins" (Acts 2:38). And when Paul was summing up his career before King Agrippa, he said that he had "declared first to those at Damascus, then at Jerusalem and throughout all the country of Judea, and also to the Gentiles, that they should repent and turn to God and perform deeds worthy of their repentance" (Acts 26:20). So, whether to Jew or Gentile, the proclamation of the gospel confronted people with the gracious act of God in their behalf and demanded decision. Since God's action was deliverance from sin, to accept it meant to turn away from sin and to believe in what God had done. When, however, through repentance and faith one enters the community of the repentant and the faithful and becomes a member of the "people of God," his or her new life must be worked out in every relationship. One's own mind, feelings, and will must be brought into conformity to new life, as well as all relationships to other people and to the world. This means that although the gospel is not a philosophy nor a theology nor an ethic, it involves philosophy, theology, and ethics. The whole of life must be bent to the summons: "Work out your own salvation with fear and trembling; for God is at work in you, both to will and to work for his good pleasure" (Phil 2:12-13). Study, struggle, discipline, costly adventure—these are all necessary in trying to discover what the "good pleasure" of God is in every phase of individual and corporate life.

Hence, the Christian never attains, but is always "press[ing] on toward the goal for the prize of the upward call of God in Christ Jesus" (Phil 3:14). The Christian is ever striving toward "mature manhood, to the measure of the stature of the fullness of Christ" (Eph 4:13), so that one's "manner of life" may "be worthy of the gospel of Christ" (Phil 1:27). A lifetime is not sufficient to work out all the implications for life of the simple facts of God's gracious action in our behalf in Christ. But these implications are not the faith, they are its expression. It has been said that "by their fruits ye shall *know*" Christians, but not produce them (Matt 7:20). They are produced only by faith in the redemptive events. Christian behavior is the outgrowth of Christian faith.

The Final Manifestation of Jesus' Lordship

One aspect of the church's faith has been largely blotted out for the average Christian in our day—the ultimate victory of Christ at his final appearing. It has become fashionable to say that one is so much interested in Jesus' first coming that he has no interest in his second coming. Furthermore, many have avoided the doctrine of the second coming because of the excesses of those who have lifted it out of its biblical perspective and have tried to predict events and determine dates. It is true that an abundance of folly has been perpetrated on the world in the name of the second coming of Christ. But the perversion of a doctrine is no justification for its abandonment. The fact remains that the reappearing of Christ is too deeply imbedded in the N Test records to remove it without hopelessly mutilating them.

The NT church lived in tension. Much as the early Christians believed in the glory of what Christ *had done*, they lived in hope of something he was *yet to do.* That which he had begun he would complete. Faith in what he had already accomplished in his first appearing, therefore, quickened hope in what he would do at his final appearing. Jesus was not only the fulfillment of promise, he was also the promise of fulfillment. His Lordship in which the church believed was now hidden, seen only by the eyes of faith. Since this Lordship was real, it must some day be openly manifested for all to see. What is true in the heavenly places where Christ is seated at the right hand of God must become true in the whole created universe which is in rebellion against him.

At no point is the NT more strange to our ears than in this respect. It tells us that "the kingdom of God has come upon" us (Matt 12:28), yet counsels us to pray, "Thy kingdom come" (Matt 6:10). It tells us that God has said to Jesus, "Sit at my right hand, till I make thy enemies a stool for thy feet" (Heb 1:13). In this passage the seeming contradiction is clear. To sit at God's right hand meant that Jesus was already Lord. And yet, he is to sit there to await the time when through the subduing of his enemies he will be Lord. It was almost like saying, "Be Lord, until you have become Lord." It was out of this seeming contradiction that the deathless hope of the early Christians was born. Tension between what had already happened and what was yet to happen marked their faith. Their gospel involved what God had done, what he was now doing, and what he would yet do. Living in the present, their faith turned to the past, and their hope to the future.

They felt that at the cross and the resurrection the decisive victory in God's conflict with evil was won. There Jesus was manifested as Lord. But the war is not yet ended. The struggle continues. Because the decisive battle has ended in victory, however, there is no question that the final outcome will be complete victory for Jesus. *He will complete what he has begun*! The hope of the second coming is not only the hope of his appearing. It is the hope of what he will accomplish when he appears. There will be an "end, when he delivers the kingdom to God the Father after destroying every rule and every authority and power" (1 Cor 15:24).

This victory will be not only the achievement of immortality for individual souls. It will be the final establishment of the people of God, a community of redeemed men and women who through Christ will finally have reached the purpose for which God created humans—perfect fellowship with himself and with each other. Foretastes of this are given to the church now. The gift of the Holy Spirit is a down payment on the inheritance which awaits us at the end. Something of true fellowship with God and with each other is given to the members of Christ's body. These foretastes suggest the glory that shall be given when God has completed his work in Christ in behalf of humanity. For this we hope.

This hope has a very practical value. It sustains the church when the going gets hard and when the odds seem insurmountable. In a struggle, people can fight on even to the death if they know that their fight will end in victory. When uncertainty of the outcome creeps in, however, the nerve of action is cut. The church's courage is sustained through the knowledge that she is fighting a battle which is already won. As Luther once remarked, the struggles of the church now are but a part of *the celebration of Christ's victory*. Martyrs could go to their death singing praise to Christ, thus celebrating the fact that even though they died, Jesus Christ is Lord, Lord even of the enemies who put them to death. It is this confidence alone which can sustain the church in our time, which is again put under the cross, facing enemies who would appear unconquerable were it not for the knowledge that they are already conquered.

The final victory will not come by human striving. It will be the act of God. As the first appearance of Christ came at the end of a long period of waiting and hoping on the part of the OT people of God, but was purely God's act, not humanity's achievement, so the final appearing will come not as an accomplishment of humans, but as the gift of God. The time of the end or the form it will assume are not ours to know. They are God's secret. We could not understand them if told. But the church waits in faith, working through love, with the patience of hope. She lives in the full confidence that Jesus will finally overcome, because she hears him say, "Be of good cheer, I have overcome the world" (John 16:33). As God was Lord of the old creation through all the process by which it came into being, so Christ is Lord of the new creation at every stage of its development until the end.

SOFT DIFFERENCE

Theological Reflections on the Relation Between Church and Culture in 1 Peter

MIROSLAV VOLF

GOSPEL, CULTURE, CHURCH

As much as anyone else during the past 100 years, the German theologian Ernst Troeltsch has shaped contemporary thinking on gospel and culture. To give just one example, probably the most important book on the topic in the English-speaking world, H. Richard Niebuhr's classic historical and theological study *Christ and Culture*,"in one sense undertakes no more than to supplement and in part to correct" Troeltsch's work on *The Social Teachings of the Christian Churches*.[1] Why did Troeltsch earn such a wide hearing?

Following in the footsteps of sociologist Max Weber, Troeltsch developed a very influential distinction between "church" and "sect" (and added his own third category of "mystic," which I will leave aside here because my interest is in Christian community). As Weber suggested, the distinction runs something like this: you *get born* into the church; you *join* a sect; like a good mother, the church will embrace you irrespective of your behavior; like a stern father, the sect will make you follow a strict ethical code.[2]

Weber's distinction between church and sect was supposed to be a strictly sociological distinction that provided models of how religious groups relate to the larger world. Going beyond Weber, Troeltsch made the simple but astute observation that one cannot separate theology from sociology. The church, which wishes to embrace all its sons and daughters, will invariably proclaim "grace"; the sect, to which only an elite number belong, will stress "law." The church will affirm the "world"; the sect will deny the "world" by retreating from it or occasionally attacking it. The church will seek power in the world, and to achieve it, make the necessary compromises; the sect will insist on undiluted purity and remain on the margins. The church will stress sacraments and education; the sect will value conversion and commitment.

By analyzing the teachings of church and sect through the centuries, in his magisterial *The Social Teaching of the Christian Churches* Troeltsch concluded that "the whole Christian world of thought and dogma" depends "on the fundamental sociological conditions, on the idea of fellowship which was dominant at any given time."[3] Troeltsch was no social determinist; after all he believed that the "idea" of Christianity gave rise to all three social forms—church, sect, and mystic—in which the Christian faith was lived out through the centuries. Yet these social forms in turn shaped Christian doctrine, the very center of it. For instance, the Christ of a church is different from the Christ of a sect: the first is a gracious "Redeemer" the second is a commanding "Lord." Similar kinds of differences between church and sect can be observed with respect to other doctrines too. One might disagree with Troeltsch on particular points, but his thesis as a whole makes sense. The beliefs and practices of a Christian community are inextricably bound to its character as a social reality; when you change one, sooner or later you will change the other too.

Notice the implications of Troeltsch's thesis about the interrelation of Christian communities' social forms and their doctrines and practices for the topic of gospel and culture. "Gospel" is never simply "the good news," not even the good news supported by a web of beliefs and practices. "Gospel" always involves a way of living in a given social environment as a Christian community (in a broad sense, including various degrees of commitment). To ask about how the gospel relates to culture is to ask how to live as a Christian *community* in a particular cultural context. Reflection on gospel and culture will be truncated without reflection on church and culture. Indeed, there is no other way to reflect adequately on gospel and culture except by reflecting on how the social embodiments of the gospel relate to a given culture.

Church and culture is the topic I wish to address. I want to explore the nature of Christian communal presence in contemporary societies and the character of Christian identity and difference. To that end I will engage in what might be called "theological and sociological exegesis" of one key biblical book on the topic—1 Peter. Methodologically, I will neither examine simply the text of 1 Peter nor simply the situation of the addressees, the Petrine community. Rather, I am interested in the reactions of the author to the situation. I am assuming, however, that, though absent from the community, in a profound sense the author of 1 Peter is still a part of it.

But why 1 Peter? In *Christ and Culture* Niebuhr seeks to indicate how the various types of relation between Christ and culture which he finds in the history of the church are exemplified in various texts produced by the early Christian communities. "Christ against culture" is best expressed in 1 John, "the Christ of culture" in Gnostic writings, "Christ above culture" in some motifs in Matthew's gospel (such as rendering to Caesar the things that are Caesar's), "Christ and culture in paradox" in the Pauline writings, and "Christ the transformer of culture" in the Fourth Gospel.

I should say that I find Niebuhr's typology enticing but unpersuasive, and his treatment of the NT texts is skewed. But this is not the point I wish to dwell on here. What interests me more is the observation that the one text which speaks more pointedly and comprehensively to the problem of "Christ and culture" than any other in the NT is conspicuously absent from Niebuhr's account. I am referring to 1 Peter, the epistle whose main theme is Christian life in a non-Christian environment.[4] I am not sure about reasons for this omission on Niebuhr's part. But I am quite sure that 1 Peter bursts not only Niebuhr's five neat models of how Christ relates to culture, about also Troeltsch's distinction between church and sect.

ALIENS AND SOJOURNERS

As Reinhard Feldmeier has argued recently, the key metaphor which 1 Peter employs to express the Christian relationship to culture is the metaphor of "aliens" (*paroikos* and *parepidēmos*).[5] It takes only a brief glance through the history of the church to see its potency. By the second century being "alien" had become central to the self-understanding of Christians. Later it was essential to monastic and Anabaptist movements alike, to Augustine and Zinzendorf, and, in our own time, to Dietrich Bonhoeffer (*The Cost of Discipleship*) no less than to Jim Wallis (*Sojourners*) or Stanley Hauerwas (*Resident Aliens*).

The metaphor "aliens" had such a powerful influence because it sums up central themes from the OT and expresses some fundamental perspectives from the whole NT about the problem of Christian identity and difference. Abraham was called to go from his country, his kindred, and his father's house (Gen 12:1). His grandchildren and the children of his grandchildren became "aliens in the land of Egypt" (Lev 19:34), and the nation of which he and Sarah were parents lived as exiles in the Babylonian captivity. And even when they were secure in their own land, Yahweh their God demanded of them to be different from surrounding nations.

The root of Christian self-understanding as aliens and sojourners lies not so much in the story of Abraham and Sarah and the nation of Israel as it does in the destiny of Jesus Christ, his mission and his rejection which ultimately brought him to the cross. "He came to what was his own, and his own people did not accept him" (John 1:11). He was a stranger to the world because the world into which he came was estranged from God. And so it is with his followers. "When a person becomes a believer, then he (or she) moves from the far country to the vicinity of God.... There now arises a relation of reciprocal foreignness and estrangement between Christians and the world."[6] Christians are born of the Spirit (John 3:8) and are therefore not "from the world" but, like Jesus Christ, "from God" (John 15:19).

There is no need here to give a detailed analysis of the trajectory from Abraham and the people of Israel to Jesus Christ and his church. It will suffice to take a careful look at the metaphor "aliens" in 1 Peter. Yet to understand the metaphor, an analysis of the terms *paroikos* and *parepidēmos,* say of an etymological or even sociological kind, will not do. In 1 Peter these terms mean not more and not less than *what the epistle as a whole teaches about the relation of Christians to the surrounding culture.* To unpack "aliens" we need to broaden our vision and look at what the epistle as a whole says about the nature of Christian presence in a given culture.

On the matter of Christians living in a non-Christian environment 1 Peter is not simply one little voice among other NT voices. Though the epistle is marginal within the NT as a whole, it pulls together "essential social-ethical traditions"of the NT as a whole.[7] A careful reader will, however, discover in 1 Peter not only a "compiler," but a creative thinker in his own right, capable of integrating the social features which Troeltsch tells us we should find clearly separated and assigned to different social types of religious communities.

ESCHATOLOGICAL DIFFERENCE

The designation of Christians as *paroikoi* and *parepidēmoi* (1 Pet 1:1; 2:11) implies, without a doubt, a "clear distance in relation to society, a distance from its values and ideals, from its institutions and politics."[8] What does the distance mean, however? Distance in what sense and for what reason?

In his well known sociological and exegetical study, John H. Elliott advocated a thesis that the term *paroikoi* describes the social marginalization which Christians experienced before conversion. In the church they then found a protective *oikos* and were provided with an ideological self-understanding as the new eschatological people of God.[9] The "homeless" found the warmth of an ecclesial home. That may well have been the case—provided one understands ideology in a purely functional manner, without reference to the truth content of the claims it contains.[10]

This helpful sociological perspective is, however, one-sided in a crucial respect. While it rightly perceives the estrangement which a Christian way of life—or Christian "ideology"—might help overcome, it underestimates a *new estrangement which a Christian way of life creates.*[11]That the members of the Petrine community might have become Christians because many of them were socially marginalized seems an intelligent hypothesis. That they became alienated from their social environment in a new way when they became Christians is what the episode explicitly states.[12] Before conversion, they were much like their neighbors (see 4:3ff); after conversion they became different, and this was the cause of their persecution.[13] Since our topic here is not the psycho-sociology of conversion, but the nature of *Christian* presence in the world, I will concentrate on this new distance, which arises from becoming a Christian.

It would be a mistake, however, to describe this new distance as simply *religious.* In that case, the terms "aliens" and "sojourners" would have been used purely metaphorically and would indicate "no actual social condition of the addressees."[14] Such a view would presume that religion is essentially a strictly private affair, touching only the deep region of a person's heart. Surely this is a mistaken view. That religion takes place simply between a naked soul and its divinity is a prejudice, one which is nourished today by the fact that in modern societies religion has been pushed outside of the public arena. Yet even in the so-called private sphere—such as the personal life, family or friendships—religion *continues to be a social force.*[15] Religion is essentially a way of thinking and of living within a larger social context. Religious distance from the world is therefore always social distance. At least this holds true for Christian faith.

How does this Christian distance from society that is religious and social come about? First Peter answers: through *the new birth into the living hope.* "Blessed be the God and Father of our Lord Jesus Christ! By his great mercy he has given us a new birth into the living hope through the resurrection of Jesus Christ from the dead" (1:3). The new birth, whose subject is the merciful and electing God (1:2), creates a two-fold distance. First, it is a *new* birth. It distances one from the old way of life, inherited from one's ancestors (1:18) and transmitted by the culture at large—a way of life characterized by the lack of knowledge of God and by misguided desires (1:14). Second, it is a birth into a *living hope.* It distances one from the transitoriness of the present world, in which all human efforts ultimately end in death. In more abstract theological terms, the new birth into the living hope frees people from the meaninglessness of sin and hopelessness of death.

This process of distancing by rebirth takes place through redemption by the blood of the Lamb (1:19) and through the resurrection of Jesus Christ from the dead (1:3). People who are born into the living hope take part in the eschatological process which started with the coming of Jesus Christ into this world, with his ministry of word and deed and with his death and his resurrection. Christian difference from the social environment is therefore an *eschatological* one. In the midst of the world in which they live, they are given a new home that comes from God's future. The new birth commences a journey to this home.

Notice the significance of the new birth for Christian social identity. Christians do not come into their social world from outside seeking either to accommodate to their new home (like second generation immigrants would), shape it in the image of the one they have left behind (like colonizers would), or establish a little haven in the strange new world reminiscent of the old (as resident aliens would). They are not outsiders who either seek to become insiders or maintain strenuously the status of outsiders. Christians are the *insiders* who have diverted from their culture by being born again. They are by definition those who are not what they used to be, those who do not live like they used to live. Christian difference is therefore not an insertion of something new into the old from outside, but a bursting out of the new *precisely within the proper space of the old.*

The question of how to live in a non-Christian environment, then, does not translate simply into the question of whether one adopts or rejects the social practices of the environment. This is the question outsiders ask, who have the luxury of observing a culture from a vantage point that is external to that culture. Christians do not have such a vantage point since they have experienced a new birth as inhabitants of a particular culture. Hence they are in an important sense insiders. As those who are a part of the environment from which they have diverted by having been born again and whose difference is therefore internal to that environment, Christians ask, "Which beliefs and practices of the culture that is ours must we reject now that our self has been reconstituted by new birth? Which can we retain? What must we reshape to reflect better the values of God's new creation?"

ECCLESIAL DIFFERENCE

Talk about "new birth" could suggest a purely individual process of distancing from the culture—a soul takes flight from the world, and seeks refuge with the eternal God, and becomes a stranger to the world of sin and death in that it migrates *(metoikizō)* into its undefiled and imperishable inheritance (1:4)[16] In a modern version of such individualistic faith a person would not depart from the world but would, like Sheila Larson in *Habits of the Heart,* says, "I believe in God.... My faith has carried me a long way. It's Sheilaism. Just my own little voice."[17] If this were what was meant by "new birth," Christian difference would be strictly private; gnosticism and mysticism would thrive under the name-brand "Christianity." Does the text of 1 Peter support such understandings of new birth, however?

The new birth "of the imperishable seed, through the living and enduring word of God" (1:23) is not simply an internal and private event. Think of its inextricable connection with baptism. Some exegetes surmise that the whole epistle is a baptismal liturgy.[18] Be that as it may, a connection between new birth and baptism is undeniable—a fact with momentous consequences. No one can baptize himself or herself; everyone must be baptized by another person into a given Christian community. Baptism is an *incorporation* into the body of Christ, a doorway into a Christian community. Baptism will not do the distancing for you, but it will tell you that genuine Christian distance has ecclesial shape. It is lived in a community that lives as "aliens" in a larger social environment.

The new birth is neither a conversion to our authentic inner self nor a migration *(metoikesia)* of the soul into a heavenly realm, but a translation of a person into the house of God *(oikos tou theou)* erected in the midst of the world. It comes as no surprise, then, to find in 1 Peter that OT *collective* designations for the people of God are applied to the Christian church: "But you are a chosen race, a royal priesthood, a holy nation, God's own people" (2:9). The distance from the social environment in 1 Peter is not simply eschatological; it is also *essentially ecclesiological.*[19] Its correlate is the eschatological *people of God,* who live in the world hoping for God's new creation, not "our own authentic little voice" nor some "heavenly home" separated from this world by an unbridgeable gulf.

Correspondingly, one must understand the "walk" *(anastrophē)* of Christians which 1 Peter so strongly emphasizes (1:15, 17, 18; 2:12; 3:1, 2, 16) not as private morality instructing how to purify the soul from an evil world nor how to "love yourself and be gentle with yourself. . . take care of each other,"[20] but as an *ecclesial way of being* that is distinct from the way of being of the society at large. "Walk" is the way the *Christian community* lives in the world. Wherever Christians find themselves—alone or with other believers—a Christian social difference is manifested there. Communities of those who are born anew and follow Christ live an alternative way of life within the political, ethnic, religious, and cultural institutions of the larger society.

We get no sense from 1 Peter, however, that the church should strive to regulate all domains of social life and reshape society in the image of the heavenly Jerusalem. One could argue, of course, that it would be anachronistic to expect such a thought even to occur in the Petrine community. Were they not discriminated against, a minority living in premodern times? Does that invalidate or compromise their stance, however? Why would it? Whatever the reason, the Petrine community was no aggressive sect in the sense of Ernst Troeltsch. It did not wish to impose itself or the kingdom of God on the world, but to live in faithfulness to God and to the values of God's kingdom, inviting others to do the same. It had no desire to do for others what they did not want done for them. They had no covert totalitarian agenda. Rather, the community was to live an alternative way of life in the present social setting, transforming it, as it could, from within. In any case, the community did not seek to exert social or political pressure, but to give public witness to a new way of life.

DIFFERENCE AND IDENTITY

Celsus, the most significant critic of Christianity in the second century, wrote: "If all men wanted to be Christians, the Christians would no longer want them."[21] In fact he insisted that Christians were so fascinated with rejecting what is common to all people that they themselves would no longer want to be Christians if everyone decided to become one. In his view, the primary point of reference for Christian identity was the non-Christian world. Christian identity is established through the negative activity of setting oneself apart from others. Christian distance from society is a spiteful difference for the sake of difference, nourished by a deep-seated resentment against the dominant social order which rejected them. Is this what we find in 1 Peter?

There is no doubt that 1 Peter stresses the church's difference from its social environment. This is what the metaphor "aliens" suggests and this is what surfaces repeatedly throughout the epistle.[22] But what is the significance of this observation for the nature of Christian identity? I suggest that the crucial question is not to what degree one stresses difference, but rather on what basis Christian identity is established. Identity can be forged through two related but clearly distinct processes: either through a negative process of rejecting the beliefs and practices of others, or through a positive process of giving allegiance to something distinctive. It is significant that 1 Peter consistently establishes the difference positively, not negatively. There are no direct injunctions not to behave as non-Christians do. Rather, the exhortation to be different centers primarily on the positive example of a holy God (1:15f) and of the suffering Christ (2:21ff). This is surprising, especially given the situation of social conflict in which the Petrine community was engaged. We expect injunctions to reject the ways of the world; instead we find admonitions to follow the path of Christ.

Let me reinforce this point by looking at two images of evil in 1 Peter: the *devil* and *fleshly desires*. 1 Peter does not warn in totalizing discourse against an evil world, but calls his community to resist the devil that prowls around, looking for someone to devour (5:8). The image of a prowling devil suggests that evil is not some impenetrable darkness outside the walls of the church, equally thick in all places; rather, evil is a mobile force, something one always has to deal with but is never quite sure where and how one will encounter it. The statements that celebrate Christian calling "out of darkness into his marvelous light" notwithstanding (2:9), 1 Peter does not operate with the stark black-and-white opposition between "divine community" and "satanic world." Correspondingly, the author seems less interested in hurling threats against the unbelieving and aggressive non-Christian neighbors,[23] than in celebrating Christians' special status before God (see 2:9f). Christian hope, not the damnation of non-Christians, figures centrally in the letter (see 1:3; 3:15).[24]

When we encounter negative examples of how Christians should not behave, then our attention is drawn not so much to the life-style of non-Christians as to "the *desires of the flesh* that wage war against the soul" (2:11). These are, as 1 Peter points out explicitly, the former desires of Christians themselves.[25] The force of the injunction is not "Do not be as your neighbors are!" but "Do not be as *you were!*"[26] This fits with the observation that the new birth distances people first of all from their old culturally shaped self and in this way from the world. This is what the logic of the metaphor of new birth suggests, but this is also what 1 Peter explicitly states: "you were ransomed from *your* futile ways inherited from your ancestors" (1:18). What permeates the epistle is not a fixation on distance from the world, but enthusiasm about the eschatological future.

It is Christian identity that creates difference from the social environment, not the other way around. The faith of the Petrine community is nourished more on its own intrinsic vision than on the deprecatory stories about others.[27] Let me reinforce this point by an observation. When identity is forged primarily through the negative process of the rejection of the beliefs and practices of others, violence seems unavoidable, especially in situations of conflict. We have to push others away from ourselves and keep them at a distance, and we have to close ourselves off from others to keep ourselves pure of their taint. The violence of pushing and keeping away can express itself in subdued resentment, or it can break out in aggressive and destructive behavior. The Petrine community was discriminated against and were even a persecuted minority. Feelings of rage and thoughts of revenge must have been lurking as a threat, ready to rise up either in aggression toward their enemies or at least in relishing the thought of their future damnation. But what do we find in 1 Peter? Exhortation is given not to repay evil for evil or abuse for abuse, but to *repay evil with a blessing* (3:9)! From the perspective of pop psychology or quasi-revolutionary rhetoric, such a refusal to vent the rage and actuate the mechanism of revenge would be at best described as unhealthy and at worst thought of as worthy only of "despicable rubble."[28] In fact, it speaks of sovereign serenity and sets a profound revolution in motion. When blessing replaces rage and revenge, the one who suffers violence refuses to retaliate in kind and chooses instead to encounter violence with an embrace. But how can people give up violence in the midst of a life-threatening conflict if their identity is wrapped up in rejecting the beliefs and practices of their enemies? Only those who refuse to be defined by their enemies can bless them.

DIFFERENCE AND ACCULTURATION

There is a strange tension in 1 Peter between the stress on difference and attempts at acculturation. This tension has given rise to opposing interpretations of the purpose of the letter as a whole. The dominant metaphor, "aliens," clearly underlines the difference. John H. Elliott latches onto the metaphor and argues that the main purpose of 1 Peter is to protect Christian identity in an unfriendly environment. "The Petrine strategy was," he writes, "to avert . . . forces of social disintegration through a reinforcement of the distinctive identity of the Christian community."[29] On the other hand, if one looks at the so-called "household codes" and compares them with similar material from the Hellenistic tradition, then it seems that interest in difference gives way to attempts at acculturation. David L. Balch argues that the household codes unmistakably manifest 1 Peter's interest in accommodation. He concludes: "The author of 1 Peter wrote to advise Christians who were being persecuted about how they might become socially-politically acceptable to their society."[30]

Elliott's and Balch's thought moves within the framework of the alternative: either difference or acculturation (though both are aware that both processes were going on at the same time). Behind such a stance seems to be the persuasion that the community of 1 Peter was a "sect" which, in order to survive, either had to assert itself under pressure to assimilate or accommodate under the threat of persecution. Yet why focus on alternatives? If both difference and accommodation were taking place at the same time, would it not be more fruitful to ask how the processes were combined? The focus on the combination of difference and acculturation would assume on the part of the Petrine community, however, a nonsectarian distance from their social environment: one is free from the pressure either simply to reject or simply affirm the surrounding culture.[31] Indeed, if I am right that the distance from the social environment is in 1 Peter primarily a positive one resulting less from the rejection of the world than from the experience of the new birth to a living hope, then we can expect the epistle to transcend these unhelpful alternatives. We would have to take into account the possibility of either rejecting or accommodating to particular aspects of the surrounding culture in a piece-meal fashion. This is, I think, what we actually find in 1 Peter.

In order to support this claim, I want to look at the so-called "household codes," the material which according to David L. Balch, clearly demonstrates a Petrine strategy of accommodation. I want to argue that the "household codes" in 1 Peter are in fact an example of differentiated acceptance and rejection of the surrounding culture.

If one considers only the repeated injunctions to "subordinate oneself" (2:13; 2:18; 3:1), to suffer injustice (2:19), or to be gentle and tender (3:4; 3:8), then it could seem that in 1 Peter "Greek politics" is indeed celebrating victory over "the Mosaic story of salvation," the prophetic tradition, and the teachings of Jesus, as Balch claims.[32] One should not forget, however, the social and theological context of these statements. First, in 1 Peter the conservative "Hellenistic" instructions do not pertain to the relationships within the church (as do the household codes proper in Ephesians and Colossians), but to the relationship of Christians to non-Christians.[33] Second, Christians were involved in a conflict that they did not provoke, that they could not avoid, and in which they were the oppressed party. Third, an inalienable dimension of their communal identity was a commitment to love of enemies and to nonviolence. Taken together, these three considerations place the "conservative" exhortation in a new light. To be "subject" means to act in the freedom of the slaves of God (2:16) and, instead of provoking additional acts of violence, to curb violence by doing good (knowing all along that suffering will be one's lot, because one cannot count on the victory of good over evil in this world). To be "subject" in a situation of conflict means to follow in the footsteps of the crucified Messiah and to refuse to take part in the automatism of revenge[34] —"evil for evil or abuse for abuse" (3:9)—and to break the vicious circle of violence by suffering violence. If the injunction to be subject appears at first to function as a religious legitimation of oppression, it turns out, in fact, to be *a call to struggle against the politics of violence in the name of the politics of the crucified Messiah.* How blinded must one be by the prejudices of one's own liberal culture to see in this demanding way of suffering only accommodation to the dominant norms of the Hellenistic world!

Yet even when we are ready to accept that "subjection"—in politics, economics, and in the home—can be an expression of radical Christianity rather than denial of Christian faith, we are still deeply troubled about how natural it seems for 1 Peter to accept the oppressive rule of the powerful— of the emperor and his governors (2:13ff), of the slave master (2:18ff), and of the husband (3:1ff). True, 1 Peter provides them with no theological legitimation; we read nowhere in the epistle that the powerful were placed in their positions by God and that they are doing God's work (see Rom 13:1-7). Moreover, 1 Peter is sensitive to the possible injustice of the existing order.[35] Contrary to Aristotle who believed that "there can be no injustice" toward slaves,[36] 1 Peter explicitly states that Christian slaves were suffering unjustly (2:19).

Still, we sense no desire to call into question the hierarchical and oppressive social order. Why? Is this because of the minority status of the first Christians? (How could we change anything!?) Is it because of the expectation of Jesus' imminent coming (4:7)? (Why should we bother, when God's new creation is around the corner!?) Is it because of a premodern understanding of social realities? (This is how things always were and how they always will be!) Possibly all three factors are relevant. In any case, it seems clear that 1 Peter accommodates to the existing social realities as well as calling them into question. We should keep in mind, however, that the call to follow the crucified Messiah was, in the long run, much more effective in changing the unjust political, economic, and familial structures than direct exhortations to revolutionize them would ever have been. For an allegiance to the crucified Messiah—indeed, worship of a crucified God—is an eminently political act that subverts a politics of dominion at its very core.[37]

Today, we might reason, in contemporary democratic societies we must engage the structures of oppression directly. Social structures are made by human beings and, if unjust, must be unmade by them. That we are ready to act is admirable; that we have an urge to reshape and reconfigure everything might be dangerous. Stephen Toulmin has noted in *Cosmopolis* a feature of modernity that he called "The Myth of the Clean Slate."[38] Just like one can be rational only if one "demolishes all that was there before and starts from scratch," so one can be revolutionary only if one refashions the political situation from the ground up.[39] For example, the French Revolution "reached into everything. For example, it re-created time and space. . . . [T]he revolutionaries divided time into units that they took to be rational and natural. There were ten days to a week, three weeks to a month, and twelve months to a year."[40] For modernity social change is enactment of a master narrative that the prophets of the new age have written on a clean sheet of paper.

But the notion of "the clean slate" has proven a dangerous myth. During the French Revolution and in particular later in this century we have learned by bitter experience that the slate cannot be cleaned and that in the process of trying a good deal of new dirt is generated—in fact, rivers of blood and mountains of corpses. Those lessons of history make us wonder whether some wisdom, in addition to accommodation, may be contained in 1 Peter's failure to challenge the oppressive structures of his day. What we should learn from the text is not, of course, to keep our mouths shut and hands folded, but to make our rhetoric and action more modest so that they can be more effective. As we strive for social change, 1 Peter nudges us to drop the pen that scripts master narratives and instead give account of the living hope in God and God's future (3:15; 1:5),[41] to abandon the project of reshaping society from the ground up and instead do as much good as we can from where we are at the time we are there (2:11), to suffer injustice and bless the unjust rather than perpetrating violence by repaying "evil for evil or abuse for abuse" (3:9), and to replace the anger of frustration with the joy of expectation (4:13).

SOFT DIFFERENCE

Though 1 Peter does not envisage changing social structures, Christians nevertheless have a mission in the world. They should conduct themselves "honorably among the Gentiles...so that they may see your honorable deeds and glorify God when he comes to judge" (2:12; cf. 3:1f). Indeed, the purpose of Christian existence as a whole is to "proclaim the mighty acts of him who called you out of darkness into his marvelous light" (2:9). The distance from society that comes from the new birth into a living hope does not isolate from society. For hope in God, the Creator and Savior of the whole world, knows no boundaries. Instead of leading to isolation, this distance is a presupposition of mission. Without distance, churches can only give speeches that others have written for them and only go places where others lead them. To make a difference, one must be different.[42]

The key question is how churches should think and live out their difference and their mission—both inalienable and mutually dependent dimensions of their identity. In one of the central passages in 1 Peter about the mission of the church, we come across a word that has today fallen somewhat into disrepute—the word "gentleness" or "meekness" (3:16; 3:4). As is well-known, a certain kind of meekness is a weapon of the weak. They get their way by avoiding direct confrontations and by seemingly going with the flow. One might be tempted to interpret "gentleness" in 1 Peter as a debasing strategy of the powerless—i.e., be gentle because this is the only way to achieve what you desire in a hostile world.

One can only strike the enemy with the weapon of meekness, however, if one holds in the other hand a weapon called *guile*. This is precisely the weapon 1 Peter takes out of the hands of his community (2:1f; 2:22). In place of guile, which tries to confuse the enemy by pretext (2:16), 1 Peter calls for the transparency of a pure heart (1:22). A gentleness that refuses to help itself with guile is no strategy of the weak. It is the open life-stance of the strong, who feel no need to support their own uncertainty by aggression toward others. Gentleness is the flip-side of respect for the other. It is not an accident that both are mentioned together in 3:16, where Christians are told to give an account of the hope that is in them "with gentleness and reverence."[43]

It might be appropriate to call the missionary distance that 1 Peter stresses *soft difference*. I do not mean a *weak* difference, for in 1 Peter the difference is anything but weak. It is strong, but it is not hard. Fear for oneself and one's identity creates hardness. The difference that joins itself with hardness always presents the other with a choice: either submit or be rejected, either "become like me or get away from me." In the mission to the world, hard difference operates with open or hidden pressures, manipulation, and threats. A decision for a soft difference, on the other hand, presupposes a fearlessness which 1 Peter repeatedly encourages his readers to assume (3:14; 3:6). People who are secure in themselves—more accurately, who are secure in their God—are able to live the soft difference without fear. They have no need either to subordinate or damn others, but can allow others space to be themselves. For people who live the soft difference, mission fundamentally takes the form of witness and invitation. They seek to win others without pressure or manipulation, sometimes even "without a word" (3:1).

Whether it takes place gently or not, colonization is colonization. This is how Tzvetan Todorov might react to the pursuit of mission through soft difference. "Is there not already a violence in the conviction that one possesses the truth oneself, whereas this is not the case for others," he asks rhetorically, commenting on the missionary efforts of such a friend of the Indians as Las Casas.[44] Instead of asserting the universal truth, one should strive to make the otherness of others blossom. Yet even "heightening of the other's differences" must be "guided by an emancipatory praxis that keeps the other empowered to be other,"[45] as Mark Taylor puts it. But when we ask what actually keeps others empowered to be authentically themselves, judgments about truth and error, freedom and slavery, darkness and light rush in. For unless you are willing to tolerate everything except intolerance toward everything, any notion of "emancipative praxis that keeps the other empowered to be other" involves often abstracting an authentic other from a concrete other and then affirming your abstraction while condemning the concrete other. You must abstract, for instance, from the fact that women are circumcised in a given culture before you can affirm that culture. But when you affirm the other in this way, you have not affirmed them, but your own construction of their authentic identity, a construction which entails making judgments about truth and value. And so we are back at proclaiming the truth that others do not possess. The difference is that we now do it clandestinely, whereas 1 Peter would want us to do it openly. Truth will be spoken, value judgments will be made. The question is only how—upfront or surreptitiously, with harshness or with gentleness, from a position of power or from a position of "weakness." Just as gentleness is not a mere survival strategy, so the soft difference is not simply a missionary method. Rather, the soft difference is the missionary side of following in the footsteps of the crucified Messiah. It is not an optional extra, but part and parcel of Christian identity itself. To be a Christian means to live one's own identity in the face of others in such a way that one joins inseparably the belief in the truth of one's own convictions with a respect for the convictions of others. The softness which should characterize the very being of Christians—I am tempted to call it "ontic gentleness"—must not be given up even when we are (from our own perspective) persuaded that others are either wrong or evil. To give up the softness of our difference would be to sacrifice our identity as followers of Jesus Christ.

DIFFERENCE AND COMMENSURABILITY

One is immediately struck in 1 Peter with two contrary reactions of outsiders to the soft missionary difference. On the one hand, there is angered surprise and blaspheming from non-Christians that Christians are no longer joining them "in the same excesses of dissipation" (4:4). The Christian difference is the cause of discrimination and persecution. Moreover, 1 Peter tells us, such negative reaction is to be expected from non-Christians. Christians should not be surprised by the "fiery ordeal" which they have to endure (4:12). The negative reactions of non-Christians do not rest on misunderstanding, but are rooted in the inner logic of the non-Christian constellation of values which seem incompatible with the values of Christians. On the other hand, one of the central passages in 1 Peter entertains a lively hope that precisely the Christian difference—outwardly visible in their good deeds—will cause non-Christians to see the truth and eventually convert (2:12,15; 3:1; 3:16). This expectation presupposes overlap between Christian and non-Christian constellations of values. The good works of Christians can be appreciated by non-Christians and look attractive to them.

Commensurability and incommensurability between Christian and non-Christian value patterns are so intertwined in 1 Peter that they can appear in one and the same sentence: "Conduct yourself honorably among the Gentiles, so that, through that for which they malign you as evildoers, they may see your honorable deeds and glorify God when he comes to judge" (2:11). The very actions which the Gentiles malign as evil deeds, will ultimately be recognized by them as good deeds if Christians do consistently what non-Christians malign. Non-Christians will even convert on account of these good deeds. Two seemingly contradictory reactions exist side by side! Can one reconcile them?

One way to resolve the problem is to invoke the miracle of *seeing*. Non-Christians look at the same phenomenon, but they are no longer provoked to anger because they come to it from a different perspective—the perspective of faith. Yet the miracle of seeing can happen only when one has already come to faith.[46] Consequently, coming to faith would not be the result of observing good works, but perceiving good works would be the result of coming to faith. Moreover, the presupposition of this solution is that value patterns of Christians and non-Christians are incommensurable. There are no bridges or overlaps. The only thing one can do is jump from one value system into another for no apparent reason or, possibly, out of dissatisfaction. But what is significant in 1 Peter is that commensurability and incommensurability are taking place at one and the same time, that good works themselves are both the cause of blaspheming (4:4) and the cause for glorifying God (2:12).[47] How is this possible?

The stress on Christian difference notwithstanding, the "world" does not seem a monolithic place in 1 Peter. We encounter evil people who persecute Christians and who will continue to do the same, blaspheming what is most holy to Christians (4:4,12). We come across ignorant and foolish people who will be silenced by Christian good behavior (2:15). We meet people who know what is wrong and what is right and are ready to relate to Christians accordingly (2:14). Finally, we encounter people who see, appreciate, and are finally won over to the Christian faith (2:12; 3:1).[48] Thus, the picture is more complex than just the two extreme and contrary reactions. This testifies to a sensitivity in 1 Peter for the complexity of the social environment.

Let me try to explicate the implicit understanding of the social world. The world consists of a plurality of "worlds." The values of these worlds do not form tight and comprehensive systems; they are not like balls that touch but do not connect. Rather, each of these worlds consists of a mixture of partly self-consistent and partly disparate practices and thought patterns. In addition, the worlds are in a permanent social interchange which shapes values that are partly common to the interacting social worlds, partly merely compatible, and partly contrary. An essential dimension of the interchange is the struggle for social power. In this struggle, ethical persuasions and various interests collide, not only between various parties, but also within one party or even within a single person. Jean-Françcois Lyotard paints a similar picture when he writes:

> The social subject itself seems to dissolve in this dissemination of language games. The social bond is linguistic, but is not woven with a single thread. It is a fabric formed by the intersection of at least two (and in reality an indeterminate number) of language games, obeying different rules.[49]

If we do not take too seriously the talk about the dissolution of the subject.[50] Lyotard's description of the complex social interaction seems right on target.

Notice the consequences of such a picture of the social world for the question of commensurability between value systems of discrete social groups (such as a Christian church). In such a world, one cannot speak either of the principled commensurability or of the principled incommensurability of value systems. Of course, one can imagine situations in which value systems of communities *are* fully commensurable or are completely incommensurable. But this is theory, not reality. As a rule, however, they are partly commensurable and partly incommensurable. They can even be commensurable and incommensurable at the same time, insofar as the values within one community or within one single person can be contradictory. Thus when we find commensurability and incommensurability at one and the same time in 1 Peter, we should not be too quick to accuse 1 Peter of inconsistency, but rather ask whether our urge for consistency does not skew our perception of social reality. The epistle shows remarkable and refreshing sensibility for the complexity of social realities, bursting a black and white way of thinking.

In addition to explaining the different ways in which non-Christians relate to the gospel, the complex interplay of commensurability and incommensurability suggests also that there is no single proper way for Christians to relate to a given culture as a whole. Instead, there are numerous ways of accepting, rejecting, subverting or transforming various aspects of a culture which itself is a complex pattern of symbols, beliefs, values, practices and organizations that are partly congruent with one another and partly contradictory. It seems obvious, but is in no way trite, to note that 1 Peter does not speak abstractly about the relation between gospel and culture. Much like other NT writings, the epistle does not deal explicitly with "culture" as the place of Christian presence, nor with "society" as a field of Christian responsibility.[51] But it does provide some overarching perspectives about how particular Christians in Asia Minor at a particular time should relate to their diverse neighbors. Even if we find abstractions necessary and models of relating to a culture useful, we should not lose sight of the rich diversity within any given culture and therefore of the multiple ways in which the gospel relates to it, such as being "against the culture" and "converting the culture," "subverting the culture" and in some sense being even "of the culture"—all at the same time.

CONCLUSION: CHURCH, SECT, OR SOMETHING ELSE?

After the foregoing exegetical and theological analysis of Christian identity and difference in 1 Peter, let us revisit in our conclusion the church-sect typology and ask about the nature of the Petrine community as it is portrayed in 1 Peter. It seems that, through the new birth into a living hope, a "sect" was born. And indeed, before the newborn child could take her first breath, her difference, her foreignness, was manifest. As she was growing up, there was no question that she did not quite fit into her environment.

Soon, however, she began to confuse observers by provoking uncertainty about her sectarian identity. It looked as if she did not forge her identity through rejection of her social environment, but through the acceptance of God's gift of salvation and its values. She refused to operate within the alternative "affirmation of the world" versus "denial of the world," but surprised people with strange combinations of difference and acculturation. She was sure of her mission to proclaim the mighty deeds of God for the salvation of the world, but refused to use either pressure or manipulation. Rather, she lived fearlessly her soft difference. She was not surprised by the various reactions of individuals and communities among whom she lived because she was aware of the bewildering complexity of social worlds in which values are partly the same, partly different, sometimes complementary, and sometimes contradictory. And so it gradually became clear that the child who was born again through the resurrection of Jesus Christ from the dead into a living hope was not a sect at all. The unusual child who looked like a sect, but did not act like a sect, was a Christian community—a church that can serve as a model even for us today as we reflect on the nature of Christian presence in modern, rapidly changing, pluralistic societies that resist being shaped by moral norms.

NOTES

1. H. Richard Niebuhr, *Christ and Culture* (New York: Harper & Brothers, 1951), x.

2. See Max Weber, "Die protestantischen Sekten und der Geist des Kapitalismus,"*Gesam--melte Aufsätze zur Religionssoziologie* I (Tübingen: J. C. B. Mohr [Paul Siebeck], 1963), 207-36.

3. Ernst Troeltsch, *The Social Teaching of the Christian Churches* (trans. Olive Wyon; London: George Allen & Unwin, 1931), II, 994.

4. See Leonard Goppelt, *Der erste Petrusbrief* KEK XII/1 (Göttingen: Vandenhoeck & Ruprecht, 1978), 41.

5. Reinhard Feldmeier, Die Christen als Fremde. *Die Metapher der Fremde in der Antiken Welt, im Urchristentum und im 1. Petrusbrief* (Tübingen: J. C. B. Mohr [Paul Siebeck], 1992).

6. Gustaf Stählin, "*Xenos*," *TDNT* V, 29.

7. Leonard Goppelt, "Prinzipien neutestamenlicher und systematischer Sozialethik heute," *Die Verantwortung der Kirche in der Gesellschaft*, ed. Jörg Baur et al. (Stuttgart: Calver Verlag, 1973), 16.

8. Feldmeier, *Die Christen als Fremde*, 22.

9. John H. Elliott, *A Home for the Homeless. A Sociological Exegesis of 1 Peter, Its Situation and Strategy* (Philadelphia: Fortress, 1981), 21-58, 129-132. Cf. John H. Elliott, "1 Peter, Its Situation and Strategy: A Discussion with David Balch," *Perspectives on 1 Peter*, ed. C. H. Talbert (Macon: Mercer, 1986), 67f.

10. So Elliott, *A Home for the Homeless*, 268.

11. This is a systemic one-sidedness, endemic to functionalist sociological explanations; they are unable to perceive religious beliefs and practices as independent social forces. For a critique of sociological functionalism in exegesis see John Milbank, *Theology and Social Theory. Beyond Secular Reason* (Oxford: Blackwell, 1990), 111-121.

12. Elliott recognizes this but underplays its importance. See Elliott, "1 Peter, Its Situation and Strategy. . . ."

13. In persecution both the issue of difference and of justice is involved. In 1 Peter persecution is first of all a problem of difference—they became Christians and as a consequence encountered "blaspheming" and were subjected to "fiery ordeal" (4:4, 12). Injustice here seems secondary to the difference, a result of the intolerance toward "the other" and of the attempt to suppress its difference.

14. A view rightly criticized by Elliott, *Home for the Homless*, 131. Elliott seems to assume, however, that if the terms "aliens" and "sojourners" are not meant metaphorically, they must describe the social situation of Christians before conversion. But there is no reason why they could not describe their social situation *after* conversion.

15. For a brief analysis of the discussion on privatization of religion see Hubert Knoblauch, "Die Verflüchtigung der Religion ins Religiöse: Thomas Luckmans Unsichtbare Religion," in Thomas Luckmann, *Die Unsichtbare Religion* (Frankfurt a.M.: Suhrkamp, 1991), 19ff.

16. For "migration" as a philosophical category see Peter Sloterdijk, *Weltfremdheit* (Frankfurt a. M.: Suhrkamp, 1993), 80ff.

17. Robert Bellah et al., *Habits of the Heart. Individualism and Commitment in American Life* (New York: Harper & Row, 1985), 221.

18. For a discussion see J. N. D. Kelly, *A Commentary on the Epistles of Peter and Jude* (New York: Harper & Row, 1969), 15ff.

19. So also Feldmeier, *Die Christen als Fremde*, 188.

20. Bellah, *Habits of the Heart*, 221.

21. Celsus in Origen, *Contra Celsum* 3,5.7.9

22. See Elliott, *A Home for the Homeless*, 120.

23. Talk about judgment in 4:17 is not a proof to the contrary. Peter writes: "For the time has come for the judgment to begin with the household of God; if it begins with us, what will be the end of those who do not obey the gospel of God?" Notice, however, that the church as the house of God is not spared judgment. Judgment is here an inclusive, not an exclusive, category. It

is interesting to observe in this context that 1 Peter comes closest of all NT writings to entertaining the possibility that deceased non-Christians might be able to make a decision for Christ after death (4:6; Goppelt, *Der erste Petrusbrief*, 277f.).

24. See Norbert Brox, *Der erste Petrusbrief* (EKK 21; Zürich/Neukirchen Vluyn: Benzinger/Neukirchener, 1979), 16. The cryptic passage in which we are told that non-Christians were "destined" to disobey the word points, however, in a different direction (2:8).

25. See Goppelt, *Der erste Petrusbrief*, 117.

26. One can read 1 Peter 4:2 as an exhortation not to live like the non-Christians: ". . .so as to live for the rest of your earthly life no longer by human desires but by the will of God." The text speaks, however, about "*human* desires" inclusively, not of the desires of the "world" or of the non-Christians, though these desires are "the desires of the flesh" (2:11) and therefore the desires that Christians "formerly had" (1:14). Moreover, not living by human desires depends on the *positive* injunction to arm "yourself also with the same intention" as Christ (4:1). First Peter transcends the simple schema of "pure church" versus "sinful world"; the desires do not simply reign among non-Christians, but also wage war against the souls of Christians (see 2: 11).

27. On this distinction see the brief (and somewhat too stark) comments of Charles Taylor, "Comparison, History, Truth," *Myth and Philosophy*, ed. F. Reynolds and David Tracy (New York: SUNY, 1990), 54.

28. See Karl Marx, *Karl M arx/ Friedrich Engels Werke* (Berlin: Dietz Verlag, 1978), IV, 200.

29. Elliott, *A Home for the Homeless*, 217.

30. David L. Balch, *Let Wives Be Submissive. The Domestic Code in I Peter* (SBLMS 26; Chico: Scholars Press, 1981), 88. Balch later qualifies his position to mean that acculturation is the purpose of the household codes only, not of the letter as whole (see David L. Balch, "Hellenization/ Acculturation in 1 Peter," *Perspectives on 1 Peter*, ed. C. H. Talbert [Macon: Mercer, 1986], 82).

31. In the case of simple rejection one would fall into what psychologists call "negative dependence" and in the case of simple affirmation one would not yet be free from "positive dependence." In both cases behavioral patterns would be determined from the outside.

32. Balch, *Hellenization/Acculturation in 1 Peter*, 97f.

33. So Feldmeier, *Die Christen als Fremde*, 161.

34. See Hanah Arendt, *The Human Condition* (Chicago: The University of Chicago Press, 1958), 240f.

35. Feldmeier, *Die Christen als Fremde*, 162, 166.

36. Aristotle, *Nicomachean Ethics*, 11134b 9ff.

37. Carl Schmitt, *Politische Theologie II. Die Legende von der Erledigung jeder Politischen Theologie* (Berlin: Duncker & Humbolt, 1970), 118, n. 3. Cf. Jürgen Moltmann, "Theologische Kritik der Politischen Religion," J. B. Metz/J. Moltmann/W. Oelmüller, *Kirche im Prozess der Aufklärung. Aspekte einer neuen "politischen Theologie"* (München: Kaiser, 1970), 11-51; Jürgen Moltmann, "Covenant oder Leviathan? Zur Politischen Theologie der Neuzeit," *ZThK* 90 (1993), 299-317.

38. Stephen Toulmin, *Cosmopolis: The Hidden Agenda of Modernity* (New York: The Free Press, 1990), 175ff.

39. Ibid., 176.

40. Robert Darton cited by Toulmin, *Cosmopolis*, 175f.

41. For a postmodern critique of master narratives see Jean-François Lyotard, *The Postmodern Condition: A Report on Knowledge*, trans. G. Bennington and B. Massumi (Minneapolis: University of Minnesota Press, 1984), 31ff. I am more persuaded by his critique than by his proposal, however.

42. From the principle "no mission without difference," does not follow the quantitative principle "the bigger the difference, the more effective mission will be" (so K. H. Schelkle, *Die Petrusbriefe. Der Judasbrief* [HThK XIII/2; Freiburg: Herder, 1961], 72).

43. Goppelt, *Der erste Petrusbrief*, 237, suggests that *phobos* in 3:16 refers to fear before God and points to other instances in which the word is used with this meaning in 1 Peter (1:17; 2:18; 3:2). Even if one follows his interpretation in these other instances (as I think one should), the context in 3:16 points clearly towards respect for other people rather than reverence before God (see Brox, *Der erste Petrusbrief*, 160).

44. Tzvetan Todorov, *The Conquest of America: The Question of the Other*, trans. R. Howard (New York: Harper Perennial, 1984), 168.

45. Mark Kline Taylor, "Religion, Cultural Plurality, and Liberating Praxis: In Conversation with the Work of Langdon Gilkey," *The Journal of Religion* 71 (2, 1992), 162.

46. So rightly from his perspective Goppelt, *Der erste Petrusbrief*, 160.

47. It could be suggested that we try to resolve the tension between angered surprise and the embracing of Christian faith by appealing to the passage of time. At first the Gentiles are angry and then, after longer observation of honorable Christian living, they have to admit their error. But if the tension could be resolved in this way, then Christians could not see discrimination and persecution as something natural, but would have to be surprised at its persistence. But according to 1 Peter Christians should consider persecution natural (see 4:12).

48. Elliott seems to want to harmonize all these reactions and ascribe them to non-Christians monolithically understood (see "1 Peter, Its Situation and Strategy", 69).

49. Lyotard, *The Postmodern Condition*, 40.

50. For a critique of the postmodern dissolution of the subject see Alasdair MacIntyre, *Three Rival Versions of Moral Enquiry: Encyclopaedia, Genealogy, and Tradition* (Notre Dame: University of Notre Dame Press, 1990), 196ff.

51. So rightly Brox, *Der erste Petrusbrief*, 18.

ECCLESIOLOGY AND ETHICS IN 1 CORINTHIANS

RICHARD B. HAYS

I. PAUL AND COMMUNITY FORMATION

Paul was a planter of churches (1 Cor 3:6-9), an organizer of far-flung little communities around the Mediterranean that united clusters of disparate people in the startling confession that God had raised a crucified man, Jesus, from the dead and thus initiated a new age in which the whole world was to be transformed. The letters of Paul that survive in the NT are his pastoral communications with these mission outposts. Though separated from them, he continued to offer them exhortation and counsel about how to conduct their common life "worthily of the gospel of Christ" (Phil 1:27).

These general observations about the Pauline mission merely restate common knowledge, but their implications for Pauline ethics have not been sufficiently appreciated. I would like to draw particular attention to their significance for interpreting the moral vision of the Pauline letters. It will be my contention that Pauline ethics is fundamentally ecclesial in character and that we begin to grasp his moral vision only when we understand that he sees the church as inheriting the corporate vocation of God's covenant people, Israel. Apart from this foundational assumption, Paul's ethic can only appear to be what many critics have thought it to be: a haphazard conglomeration of moral notions drawn eclectically from the commonplaces of his time.

To be sure, Paul nowhere sets forth a systematic presentation of "Christian ethics." Nor does he offer his communities a "Manual of Discipline," a comprehensive summary of community organization and duties.[1] Instead, he responds *ad hoc* to the contingent pastoral problems that arise in his churches.[2] Should Gentile believers be circumcised? Should converts to Paul's movement divorce their unbelieving spouses? Or, on the other hand, should married couples who convert stop having sexual relations? Are Christians obligated to obey the Roman authorities? What is to be done when some members of the church hog all the food at the potluck supper? In every case, Paul offers answers.

The advice that he offers is not merely generic and conventional, as though he were a first-century Ann Landers, answering everybody's cards and letters in terms of a lowest common denominator of common sense. Rather, he is seeking to shape the life of a particular community in accordance with his vision; his exhortations are aimed at defining and maintaining a corporate identity for his young churches, which are emphatically countercultural communities. Thus, his letters should be read primarily as instruments of community formation. Their rhetoric consistently aims at reinforcing group cohesion and loyalty within the community of faith. Social-scientific approaches to Paul's correspondence have helpfully highlighted this aspect of his apostolic project.[3]

Paul's strong thematic emphasis on community is not, however, merely a matter of practical expediency, nor is it to be understood solely in terms of sociological models. Rather, Paul develops his account of the new community in Christ as a fundamental theological theme in his proclamation of the gospel.[4] Indeed, the focus on community is a part of the gospel itself. How so? If we ask, "What is God doing in the world in the interval between resurrection and parousia?" the answer must be given, for Paul, primarily in ecclesial terms: God is at work through the Spirit to create communities that prefigure and embody the reconciliation and healing of the world. The fruit of God's love is the formation of communities that confess, worship, and pray together in a way that glorifies God (see, e.g., Rom 15:7-13). Such communities are palpable signs of God's reconciliation of the world.

This message finds its most remarkable expression in 2 Cor 5:14-21, in which Paul declares that the death of Christ has brought into being a "new creation," made manifest in the church which is entrusted with "the ministry of reconciliation."[5] The conclusion of the passage articulates a mystery that stands at the heart of Paul's gospel: *"For our sake he made him to be sin who knew no sin, so that in him we might become the righteousness of God"* (2 Cor 5:21). Notice that he does not say "so that we might *know about* the righteousness of God" or even "so that we might *receive* the righteousness of God," or "so that we might have the righteousness of God imputed to us vicariously." Instead, the vocation of the community is to *become* the righteousness of God, to embody God's righteousness (i.e., his covenant faithfulness) in the world.[6] That was the purpose for which Christ died. The theological claim here about the identity of the church is extraordinary, but it is foundational in Paul's thought. Such a claim is possible only because Paul understands the church to be God's new covenant people, those who bear God's name and disclose his true will and character.[7]

How does this emphasis on community formation as the *telos* of God's redemptive activity cash out in Pauline ethics? What are the ethical implications of Paul's ecclesiology?

1. Those who are baptized, Paul insists, have become "one in Christ Jesus," no longer divided by former distinctions of ethnicity, social status, or gender (Gal 3:28). Because in Christ they are all "sons[8] of God," they all belong together in a single family in which all are joint heirs.[9] His passionate opposition to Cephas at Antioch (Gal 2:11-21) sprang from his urgent conviction that Jews and Gentiles must be one in Christ, not separated by social barriers. The basic problem with the desire of Jewish Christians to maintain Torah observance was, according to Paul, not that it engendered "works righteousness," but rather that it fractured the unity of the community in Christ.[10] John Barclay, following J. D. G. Dunn and others, has well summarized the ethical issue at stake: "The problem here is not legalism (in the sense of earning merit before God) but cultural imperialism—regarding Jewish identity and Jewish customs as the essential tokens of membership in the people of God."[11]

2. It is important to realize, however, that Paul could equally be accused of promulgating a reverse "cultural imperialism." He has relativized and disqualified the distinctively Jewish signs of membership in God's covenant community ("works of law"= circumcision, food laws, sabbath observance), but he has at the same time inevitably set up new marks of participation in that community (confession of faith, baptism, experience of the Holy Spirit). Daniel Boyarin, in an important and provocative study of Paul, describes Paul's vision of community as "particularist universalism."[12] It should not be

forgotten that the community whose unity Paul passionately seeks is not the human community as a whole, nor is it a pluralistic community within the *polis*. Rather, it is always the particular community of the church. To be sure, Paul hopes for the ultimate triumph of God's grace over all human unbelief and disobedience (Rom 11:32; Phil 2:9-11). Consequently, he hopes for the final reconciliation of all humanity to God. Until that eschatological consummation, however, Paul speaks only to the community of faith. He articulates no basis for a general ethic applicable to those outside the church.

3. The key questions for Pauline ethics, then, must always be formulated in ecclesial terms. *The community is the primary addressee of God's imperatives.* If the biblical story focuses on God's design for forming a covenant people—as Paul believes it does[13]—then the primary sphere of moral concern is not the character of the individual, but the corporate obedience of the church. Paul's formulation in Rom 12:1-2 encapsulates the vision: "Present your bodies [*somata*, plural] as a living sacrifice [*thysian*, singular], holy and well-pleasing to God. And do not be conformed to this age, but be transformed by the renewing of your mind...." The community, in its corporate life, is called to embody an alternative order that stands as a sign of God's redemptive purposes in the world. This is the concrete social manifestation of the righteousness of God. The coherence of Paul's ethical teaching comes into focus only when we understand that he is consistently formulating the ethical mandate in *ecclesial* terms, seeking God's will not by asking first, "What should I do?" but" What should we, as God's people, do?"

4. If indeed the church is interpreted as the proleptic fulfillment of the scriptural narrative of election and promise, one more crucial theological affirmation—alluded to already above—must be underscored: the church is the community of the new covenant. In 2 Cor 3:16, Paul explicitly describes himself as a minister of "a new covenant, not of letter but of spirit." The word of God—mediated through Paul (v.3)—is now written upon the hearts of the community, as Jeremiah had prophesied (Jer 31:33). No longer is God's will written on stone or in ink; it is embodied in the life of the community. Indeed, it was a salient aspect of Jeremiah's prophecy that no merely written law would be necessary in God's new covenant, nor would there be a need for specially authorized interpreters: *"No longer shall each man teach his neighbor and each his brother...for they shall all know me, from the least of them to the greatest."* This notion that the people of the new covenant should already know the law written on their hearts is, of course, the source of a great deal of trouble for Paul, but it also explains a great deal about his ethical *modus operandi*. He refuses to deal with ethical problems solely through exposition of the law, for he prefers to appeal to a spiritual discernment that is operative through the transformation of the community. With transformed minds, the church should be able to discern the will of God (Rom 12:2).

5. Another consequence of construing the church as the community of the new covenant is that the Pauline Gentile churches are seen in metaphorical continuity with Israel. Paul refers to Abraham as their father (Rom 4) and, writing to the predominantly Gentile church at Corinth, calls Israel of the exodus generation "our fathers in the wilderness" (1 Cor 10:1).[14] Because the continuity is metaphorical rather than "in the flesh," Paul can reject the mandate for observance of specific Torah practices such as circumcision and food laws, while retaining the claim that the community (the *ekklēsia*) is the sphere of God's special activity and blessing, the manifestation of God's righteousness.

II. THE ROLE OF ECCLESIOLOGY IN STUDIES OF PAULINE ETHICS

In light of the above summary of the ecclesial basis and orientation of Pauline ethics, it is reasonable to ask whether this aspect of Paul's thought has been appropriately recognized in NT scholarship. A full report of the research on this issue would expand this essay beyond reasonable limits, but a few general observations about the state of the question may be ventured.

1. The standard surveys of NT ethics almost completely ignore the ecclesial context and shaping of Paul's moral vision. Here I refer to the works on NT ethics by J. L. Houlden, J. T. Sanders, Allen Verhey, Siegfried Schulz, Wolfgang Schrage, L. William Countryman, Eduard Lohse, and Willi Marxsen.[15] To be sure, most of these works discuss "love" as a central theme of Paul's ethic, but they tend to treat it as though it were an individual character attribute or responsibility.

For example, J. T. Sanders writes:

> In his bondage to the flesh, the Christian cannot love; but, in the new existence granted to him in faith, and which is shortly to be actualized by God's coming, he can love or, at least, be commanded to love—that is, to attest the existence which he knows, in faith, to be his.[16]

In the succeeding paragraph, Sanders describes Rom 12:1ff. as a passage that "intends to be instructive regarding what *a Christian* is to do."[17] Remarkably, his entire discussion of Romans 12 offers no hint that Paul is addressing the community or that the passage's moral admonitions are to be lived out in the context of the *church*.[18] Indeed, Sanders can summarize Paul's basic moral intent, without reference to the community of faith, by saying that "The Christian is one who 'does the good' to his fellow man."[19] Similarly, Lohse can write of Paul's ethic in terms of "new creation in the the life of *the believer*," without any acknowledgement that for Paul the new creation is manifest precisely in the life of the community.[20]

In one sense, it is not inappropriate to apply Paul's admonitions to the life of the individual believer. Certainly Paul does think that individual Christians are called to love and that individuals participate in the new creation. My point, however, is that these general discussions of Pauline ethics employ a highly individualistic hermeneutical filter that strains out crucially important matters. Paul's concern for the life of the community is hermeneutically converted into moral exhortation for individual religious subjects. It is tempting to blame this individualistic reading on Rudolf Bultmann's influential treatment of Paul in his *Theology of the New Testament*,[21] but the truth is that Bultmann's work is also a symptom rather than a cause of the misreading that I am describing, which is rooted deep in the traditions of Western Protestantism.[22]

2. Some of the monographs that deal specifically with Pauline ethics are more helpful in calling attention to the ecclesial dimensions of Paul's moral vision. Victor Furnish's landmark study *Theology and Ethics in Paul* offers a number of clear articulations of the point that I am emphasizing:

> The conception of salvation as an individual matter between man and God is utterly foreign to Paul's preaching. . . . To be in Christ, in the Lord, in the Spirit means to be in the *community* of Christ, the Lord, and the Spirit.[23]

Hence, the will of God is always to be discerned by and for the community, not by individuals in isolation:

> This *communal* context of the believer's life is of the greatest importance for Paul's understanding of how the Christian is able to know what he ought to and ought not to do. . . . The believer's life and action are always in, with, and for "the brethren" in Christ. For him, moral action is never a matter of an isolated actor choosing from among a variety of abstract ideas on the basis of how inherently "good" or "evil" each may be. Instead it is always a matter of choosing and doing what is good for the brother and what will upbuild the whole community of brethren.[24]

Despite these forceful statments, however, Furnish does not treat ecclesiology as one of the"root-motifs" of Pauline ethics; instead, he gives programmatic emphasis to Paul's *"theological, eschatological,* and *christological* convictions."[25] In fact, apart from the passages just cited, ecclesiology plays a relatively minor role in Furnish's account of Pauline ethics.

Three studies that do place fundamental emphasis on the centrality of the church in Paul's thought are Robert Banks, *Paul's Idea of Community,* T. J. Deidun, *New Covenant Morality in Paul,* and J. Paul Sampley, *Walking between the Times.*[26] Banks' work is an exemplary elucidation of Pauline thought that has not received the attention it deserves in Pauline scholarship.[27] Deidun places entirely too much weight on a questionable exegesis of 1 Thess 4:1-12 as an articulation of "new covenant morality," but his stress on the theme of the new covenant as "the *Mitte* of pauline theology"[28]—even if slightly overdrawn—is a helpful corrective calling attention to a major neglected theme of Pauline thought.[29] Finally, Sampley offers a treatment of Pauline ethics that accords significant emphasis to the role of the community in Paul's thought. The first chapter in his section on Paul's "moral reasoning" is entitled"The Community as Primary Context,"[30] and Sampley consistently stresses the ecclesial dimensions of Paul's processes of moral deliberation.[31]

3. Studies of the social history and organization of the Pauline churches, though not dealing either with "ecclesiology" or with "ethics" as theological loci, nonetheless have contributed enormously valuable insights on our topic. Here the seminal works are those of Gerd Theissen and Wayne Meeks.[32] Meeks devotes a substantial chapter to "The Formation of the *Ekklēsia,"*[33] and his subsequent chapters on "Governance," "Ritual," and "Pattems of Belief and Pattems of Life" all contribute to an account of the church communities that Paul formed. By concentrating particularly on the setting of the Pauline communities within Greco-Roman culture, however, Meeks underplays the importance of Paul's conviction that the church is to be understood in continuity with Israel as God's elect people.

This brief survey is by no means comprehensive, but it suggests some major areas that merit further attention in our effort to understand Paul's theology and ethics. While several studies of Pauline ethics have noted the importance of the church as the context for Paul's moral vision, this insight does not seem to have impressed itself on the field of NT studies at large. The majority of studies on Paul's thought still tend to treat him as concerned with the moral choices and responsibilities of the individual believer. A classic expression of this perspective is provided by Hans Dieter Betz, whose major critical commentary on Galatians characterizes the ethical message of the letter's parenetic section (Gal 5:1-6:10) in the following way:

> ...Paul does not provide the Galatians with a specifically Christian ethic. The Christian is addressed as an educated and responsible person. He is expected to do no more that what would be expected of any other educated person in the Hellenistic culture of the time.[34]

Betz's claim that Paul provides no "specifically Christian ethic" is closely linked to his misleading assumption that Paul's moral advice is addressed to the individual Christian rather than to the church as a corporate entity which is called to "bear one another's burdens and so fulfill the law of Christ" (Gal 6:2).[35]

Since Paul continues to be read—against the grain—as preoccupied with the individual's relationship to God and with the moral responsibilty of individuals, there is a need for fresh theological studies that highlight the importance of ecclesiology (i.e., community formation) for Paul's ethics. In the remainder of this essay, therefore, I propose to reexamine a single Pauline letter (1 Corinthians) with this heuristic question in mind: how is Paul's ethic shaped by his vision of the church?

III. ECCLESIOLOGY IN THE ETHICAL ARGUMENTS OF 1 CORINTHIANS: A SURVEY

The result of reviewing 1 Corinthians through this ecclesial heuristic question is striking: the letter can be read from start to finish as the outworking of an ecclesiologically-centered ethic.[36] The Corinthians have understood the gospel in terms of *individual* spiritual fulfillment, and this misunderstanding has led to rivalry and fragmentation of the community. At every point in his response, Paul recalls them to unity by stressing the *ecclesial* context of God's grace, the corporate character of God's redemptive work in Christ, and the shared vocation of the community. Concern for unity of the community is the fundamental theme of 1 Corinthians, the common thread that binds the letter's diverse pastoral admonitions together.[37] Let us consider some representative passages.

A. *1 Corinthians 1-4: An Appeal for Unity.*

The letter's introductory thanksgiving concludes with the affirmation: "God is faithful; by him you were called into the *koinōnia* of his Son, Jesus Christ our Lord" (1 Cor 1:9). This call to the fellowship of Jesus then in turn becomes the immediate ground of a plea for unity:

> Now I appeal to you brothers and sisters, through the name of our Lord Jesus Christ, that all of you might be in agreement and that there be no divisions *(schismata)* among you, but that you be ordered in the same mind and in the same opinion (1:10) .

This exhortation is necessary because Paul has received word that there are indeed quarrels within the Corinthian community. Some of the particular causes of these divisions are discussed during the course of the letter. Paul, however, regards such disunity in the church as contrary to the word of the cross (1:18-2:5) and as a sign of the Corinthians' immaturity in the faith.

> And so, brothers and sisters, I was not able to speak to you as spiritual people, but rather as fleshly people, as infants in Christ. I gave you milk to drink, not solid food, for you were not yet able to handle it. Even now you

> are not able to handle it, for you are still fleshly. *For where there is jealousy and quarreling among you, are you not fleshly and are you not walking according to human inclinations?* (3: 1-4)

Dissension in the church is deeply worrisome to Paul, for the aim of his apostolic labors has been to build community, not just to save souls. He has "laid the foundation" (3:11), and he is concerned that other contractors are botching the subsequent construction job. The quality of construction matters urgently because the community is "God's building"(3:10). Indeed, Paul dares to assert more: the community is the place where God dwells. "Do you not know," he asks, "that you [*plural*] are God's temple and that God's Spirit dwells in you [*plural*]?"(3:16). To read this last sentence as though it spoke of the Spirit dwelling in the body of the individual Christian would be to miss the force of Paul's audacious metaphor: the apostolically founded community takes the place of the Jerusalem temple as the place where the glory of God resides.[38] When the community suffers division, the temple of God is dishonored. But the presence of the Spirit in the community should produce unity rather than conflict. Thus, the first four chapters of the letter focus on Paul's appeal for unity, not, e.g, on Paul's apostolic self-defense.

B. *A Test Case: Idol-Meat (1 Cor 8:1-11:1).*

A careful examination of 1 Cor. 8:1-11:1 will demonstrate how Paul's appeal for unity within the *ekklesia* works in response to a particular issue. The Corinthians have written to Paul about several matters (1 Cor 7:1), including the problem of food sacrificed to idols (8:1, 4). In Greco-Roman culture, a person who offered a sacrifice to the god in a pagan temple would often invite family members and friends to share in a feast at which the meat of the sacrificial animal was consumed; the feast was held in the temple of the god (cf. 8:10). In some respects, such social occasions were more like dinner parties than religious ceremonies, but their association with the pagan gods would surely have made many Jews and Christians uneasy about participating. The temptation to participate would have been strong, however, because of social pressure to conform to normal cultural practice. Furthermore, public distribution of meat was sometimes made in conjunction with civic religious festivals; such occasions were among the relatively few opportunities many people would have had to eat meat.[39] Some of the Corinthians, confident in their knowledge (*gnosis*) that "there is no idol in the world" and that "there is no God but one" (8:4) have decided that there is no harm in participating in such meals celebrated in connection with pagan religious observances. Others, however, whom Paul calls "the weak" (8:7) are scandalized by this behavior or—what Paul considers worse— drawn by the example of the "strong"[40] to join in such temple meals despite their own scruples (8:7, 10; cf. Rom 14:23: "Those who have doubts are condemned if they eat, because they do not act from faith; for whatever does not proceed from faith is sin").

Remarkably, Paul does not seek to settle the disagreement among the Corinthians by issuing a simple ruling on the disputed point. Instead, he appeals to those who do possess "knowledge" to act in loving acknowledgment of their familial interdependence with their brothers and sisters in the community who do not share their convictions. His counsel is already implied in the pithy comment with which he leads off the discussion of the problem: "Knowledge puffs up; love builds up (*oikodomei*) (8:1b; cf.10:23-24). Those who insist on their own spiritual prerogatives and refuse to place concern for the community first are pursuing a disastrous course: "So by your knowledge the weak one is destroyed, the brother for whom Christ died"(8:11). The alternative is a way of life that surrenders freedom and prerogatives for the spiritual welfare of others. Paul declares his own intention to choose this way: "Therefore, if food causes my brother to fall, I will never eat meat, so that I may not cause my brother to fall" (8:13).

This formulation provides the transition into an extended discussion of Paul's own apostolic conduct as an example of the self-surrendering behavior that he is recommending (9:1-27). As an apostle, Paul asserts, he has the right to receive financial support for his ministry; indeed, "the Lord (Jesus) commanded that those who proclaim the gospel should get their living by the gospel"(9:14; cf. Matt 10:10; Luke 10:7). Nonetheless—contrary to the direct authority of the tradition of Jesus' teaching!—he refuses to accept support, in order to "make the gospel free of charge" (9:18). The operative norm here is relinquishment of self-interest for the benefit of others.

Paul restates and generalizes this norm in 9:19-23, a passage that bears a striking structural similarity to the Philippians hymn. "For though I am free from all," he declares, "I enslaved myself to all,[41] in order that I might gain more of them"(9:19). The passage is often read as a statement of Paul's cultural flexibility for the sake of his mission; rightly so, but its deeper point is Paul's willingness to relinquish his own freedom for the sake of the gospel. With a telling self-description he signals that he has not forgotten the idol-meat issue: "To the weak I became weak, so that I might gain the weak"(9:22). That is, of course, precisely what he wants the "strong" Corinthians to do: to become weak. He is offering himself as a model for imitation. Because he presents himself as one "not seeking my own advantage, but that of many"(10:33), he can at last articulate the exhortation that undergirds the entire idol-meat discussion: "Become imitators of me, as I am of Christ."

Thus, we see that Paul addresses this pastoral problem at Corinth not by seeking to determine the appropriate halakah in Torah,[42] not by pointing to the authoritative teaching of Jesus or the pronouncement of an Apostolic Council (Acts 15), but by urging the strong members of the Corinthian church to follow the example of Christ and the example of the apostle by surrendering their place of privilege. The *telos* of such action is not just to enhance personal virtue and humility, but also to secure the unity of the *ekklēsia* in Christ. At the same time, the community is called to discern the right action in light of the story of Israel in the wilderness. The *ekklēsia* stands in a typological relation to Israel and must therefore beware the dangers of idolatry and spiritual complacency. For the church to see itself prefigured in the story of Israel is to recognize the communal imperative to "flee from the worship of idols"(10:14). The strong Corinthians see the idol-meat issue in terms of *individual* capacities and prerogatives. Paul reframes the questions as part of a narratively ordered ecclesiology, so that the issue becomes the *whole church's* freedom from spiritual compromise.

The ethical norm, then, is not given in the form of a predetermined rule or set of rules for conduct; rather, the right action must be *discerned* on the basis of a christological paradigm, with a view to the need of the community and the community's identity as God's covenant people.

C. *Community Discipline (1 Cor 5:1-6:11).*

Paul's reluctance to specify narrow behavioral norms was perhaps one of the factors that led to trouble in the Corinthian community. Acting in light of their own spiritual discernment, some of the Corinthians were acting in ways that Paul found deeply objectionable. In 1 Cor 5:1-5, for example, he condemns an incestuous relationship between a man and his mother-in-law as "sexual immorality of a kind that is not found even among Gentiles." Here he gives no reason for his rejection of this behavior; he merely pronounces condemnation. He formulates his moral indignation in a manner ("not found even among the Gentiles") suggesting that this particular normative judgment is rooted in Jewish cultural sensibilities, based ultimately on Lev 18:8: "You shall not uncover the nakedness of your father's wife." This background, however, remains implicit.

Even in this disturbing passage, however, the specific directive that Paul gives to the Corinthian church ("Drive out the evil person from among you" [5:13]) is motivated by a concern for the unitary holiness of the community: "Do you not know that a little yeast leavens the whole batch of dough? Clean out the old yeast so that you [*plural*] may be a new batch, as you really are unleavened" (5:6b-7a). Thus, concern for the health and purity of the community remains the constant factor in which more specific norms must be grounded.

Indeed, as I argued in *Echoes of Scripture in the Letters of Paul*, Paul's use of the phrase "you shall drive out the evil person from among you" in 1 Cor 5:13 directly appropriates the language of Deut 17:7 and—even more appositely—Deut 22:22, which prescribes the death penalty for illicit sexual relations among Israelites.[43] Paul thus tacitly "adopts" the Gentile Corinthians as members of the covenant people of God. His treatment of the issue makes sense only in these terms: just as Israel was to purge itself of the abominations of the inhabitants of the land, so also the church must purge itself of ways of conduct inappropriate to the kingdom of God (cf. 1 Cor 6:9-11).

Similarly, the underlying logic of Paul's rejection of recourse to the courts (6:1-8) is that disputes should be handled *within the community* of faith. To go to court before unbelievers is to breach the unity of the church. Paul's question, "Can it be that there is no *sophos* among you?" (6:5), is bitingly ironic in view of the Corinthians' claim to possess a special wisdom. True wisdom is to be found only in conduct that sustains and builds up the community.

D. *Building Up the Community through Worship.*

The ecclesial character of Paul's ethic is brought into close focus by Paul's long discussion of speaking in tongues and other spiritual gifts in the community's worship in chapters 12-14. This passage forcefully holds up the norm of communal edification as the standard by which spirituality is to be measured and guided.

Apparently some of the Corinthians were priding themselves on their rich endowments of spiritually-inspired "speech and knowledge" (cf. 1:5). In the opening of the letter Paul gives thanks, perhaps with a trace of irony, that the Corinthians "are not lacking in any spiritual gift" (1:7). He does not give a direct description of the problems surrounding spiritual manifestations in the Corinthian assembly, but his counsel suggests that some members of the community must have been claiming spiritual superiority and dominating the community's worship with virtuoso displays of glossolalia.

In responding to this situation, Paul develops an account of the church's interdependent common life:

> Now there are varieties of gifts, but the same Spirit; and there are varieties of services, but the same Lord; and there are varieties of activites, but it is the same God who activates all of them in everyone. To each is given the manifestation of the Spirit for the common good (12:4-7).

The diversity of God's gifts is necessary "for the common good" of the community. Paul underscores his point by employing the analogy of the human body in which all the parts are necessary to healthy functioning of the organism: "If one member suffers, all suffer together with it; if one member is honored, all rejoice together with it"(12:26). Then Paul introduces his foundational metaphor for the church's corporate life: "Now you are the body of Christ and individually members of it" (12:27).

Common participation in the body of Christ becomes the basis for Paul's particular directions concerning the regulation of the community's worship. Speaking in tongues is a spiritual experience, a fine thing in itself, says Paul (14:2, 5a), but it does not edify the community. All actions, however ostensibly spritual, must meet the criterion of constructive impact on the church community. Consequently, intelligible prophecy, which offers "upbuilding, exhortation, and consolation" for the community (14:3), is to be more highly valued and sought: "Those who speak in a tongue build up themselves, but those who prophesy build up the church"(14:4). The noun *oikodomē* (building up, edification) and the cognate verb *oikodomein* occur repeatedly in this chapter. The task of community building, which was originally Paul's apostolic work, is transferred to the community itself. Thus, the purpose of corporate worship becomes community formation. It is crucial, however, that the work of community-building be a shared, participatory enterprise. The worship assembly is not to be monopolized by any one member. Instead,

> When you come together, each one has a hymn, a teaching, a revelation, a tongue, or an interpretation. Let all things be done for building up *(oikodomē)* (14:26).

Thus, the gathered community's worship reflects and symbolizes the interdependence of the body of Christ.

Sandwiched between chapters 12 and 14 is Paul's great panegyric on love. Whether this is an independent piece of tradition inserted here by Paul or whether it is composed for the occasion at hand, the placement of this discourse shows that Paul interprets love in terms of the ecclesial context elaborated in the surrounding chapters. Love, rightly understood, should constrain those super-spiritual Corinthians whose behavior threatens the good of the community. Love binds the body of Christ together in mutual suffering and rejoicing; love seeks the upbuilding of the whole community rather than private advantage. It is striking that Paul places this discourse on love in the midst of his response to the tongue-speaking controversy rather than, say, in his discussion of marriage in 1 Corinthians 7. Why so? For Paul, love has its primary locus in the common life of the church.

IV. CONCLUSION: ETHICS AS ECCLESIOLOGY

What more shall I say? For time would fail me to tell of all the ways that Paul appeals to community as ethical warrant and norm in this letter. I have not yet said anything about the issue of the Lord's Supper (11:17-34), which for Paul comes down in the end to the matter of "rightly discerning the body"—i.e., recognizing that the Lord's Supper is a sign of the unity of the Body of Christ, and behaving accordingly. Nor have I yet said anything about "the collection for the saints" (16:1-4), which functions for Paul as the great symbolic enactment of the unity of Gentile and Jew, thus figuring forth the eschatological character of this new messianic community that Paul is laboring to create.

By not saying anything about these matters, I have omitted two of the most powerful expressions of the theological claim that every line of 1 Corinthians breathes forth: to discern the will of God rightly, the Corinthians must perceive their identity as the new covenant people of God, living in *koinōnia*, embodying the presence of the eschatological *Spirit of God* in a world whose previous order is passing away. The theological constant underlying Paul's counsel throughout the letter is that he imagines God's eschatological salvation in corporate terms: God transforms and saves a people, not atomized individuals. Consequently, the faithful find their identity and vocation in the world as the body of Christ.

Thus, to do "ethics" apart from ecclesiology is utterly unthinkable for Paul. Ethics is ecclesiology. Ethics is simply the church's imaginative outworking of its identity as the Israel of God.

NOTES

1. Such summaries were not uncommon in the ancient world: in various ways, the genre is represented by the Community Rule (lQS) found among the Dead Sea Scrolls, the presentation of Jesus' teaching in the Gospel of Matthew, the Didache, and the codification of Jewish halakah in the Mishnah.

2. Even the letter to Philemon, which confronts an issue that might have been considered a private pastoral matter, is addressed not just to Philemon but also to Apphia and Archippus and to "the church in your house" (Philem 2). Paul insists on laying the decision-making process open to the community's scrutiny. On the rhetorical effects of Paul's addressing the letter to the whole church, see Norman Petersen, *Rediscovering Paul: Philemon and the Sociology of Paul's Narrative World* (Philadelphia: Fortress, 1985). The Pastoral Epistles (1 and 2 Timothy and Titus) are addressed to individuals, but their authorship is debatable.

3. See especially Wayne A. Meeks, *The First Urban Christians: The Social World of the Apostle Paul* (New Haven: Yale University Press, 1983); The Moral World of the First Christians (Philadelphia: Westminster, 1986); and Bengt Holmberg, *Paul and Power: The Structure of Authority in the Primitive Church as Reflected in the Pauline Epistles* (Philadelphia: Fortress, 1980).

4 See Robert Banks, *Paul's Idea of Community: The Early House Churches in Their Historical Setting* (Grand Rapids: Eerdmans, 1980).

5. The first person plural pronouns in 2 Cor 5:18-20 may refer either to the apostle himself or to the church more generally. Although the discussion grows out of Paul's defense of his own apostolic ministry, the paragraph develops towards a climax in which the vocation of the whole church is in view, most unmistakably in v. 21. The ambiguity of reference in vv. 18-20 is a natural result of Paul's conception of the relation between his own vocation and that the community: the church is to imitate the apostle and share his vocation; conversely, the apostle models in microcosm the larger vocation of the elect people to be a light to the nations. N. T. Wright's otherwise illuminating article on this passage ("On Becoming the Righteousness of God: 2 Corinthians 5:21," in David M. Hay, ed., *Pauline Theology: Volume II: 1 & 2 Corinthians,* Minneapolis: Fortress, 1993) misses the crucial point by confining the reference of v. 21 to the apostle himself.

6.This passage should be compared to Rom 1:17, which announces that the righteousness of God "is being revealed" in the world through the gospel. In light of 2 Cor 5:21, we might well pause to ask exactly how Paul thinks that the righteousness of God is being disclosed. Is it possible that he thinks there also of the church—the body of reconciled Jews and Gentiles—as the locus of revelation? If so, Eph 2:11-22 (cf. 3:10) would be a faithful rendering of a central Pauline theme.

7. On *dikaiosunē theou* as covenant terminology, see Richard Hays, "Justification," Anchor Bible Dictionary (New York: Doubleday, 1992), 3: 1129-33.

8. Paul uses the term ηυιοι (*"huioi "*) to include both men and women, as the continuing explanation in 3:28 makes clear. The decision of the NRSVtranslators to render the term as "children" in 3:26 and 4:5-7 is hermeneutically justifiable, though it diminishes the rhetorical effect of some of Paul's turns of phrase, e.g. 4:6: "...and because you are sons, God has sent the Spirit of his Son into our hearts, crying 'Abba! Father!' "

9. Nowhere does Paul speak of all humanity as "children of God." All are God's creatures, but the language of *family* relationship is reserved for the elect community.

10. Richard B. Hays, "Christology and Ethics in Galatians: The Law of Christ," *CBQ* 49 (1987): 289-90. On the problem of why Cephas and others shunned table fellowship with Gentile converts, see E. P. Sanders, "Jewish Association with Gentiles and Galatians 2:11-14," in R. Fortna and B. R. Gaventa, eds., *The Conversation Continues: Studies in Paul and John in Honor of J. Louis Martyn* (Nashville: Abingdon), 170-188.

11. John Barclay, *Obeying the Truth: A Study of Paul's Ethics in Galatians* (Edinburgh: T. & T. Clark, 1988), 239. Barclay is building here on the insights of E. P. Sanders, *Paul and Palestinian Judaism: A Comparison of Patterns of Religion* (Philadelphia: Fortress, 1977); James D. G. Dunn, "The New Perspective on Paul," *BJRL* 65 (1983), 95-122; "The Incident at Antioch (Gal. 2:11-18)," JSNT 18 (1983), 3-57; and Francis B. Watson, *Paul, Judaism, and the Gentiles: A Sociological Approach*, SNTSMS 56 (Cambridge: Cambridge University Press, 1986).

12. Daniel Boyarin, *A Radical Jew: Paul and the Politics of Cultural Identity* (Berkeley: University of California Press, 1994).

13. I have argued elsewhere *(Echoes of Scripture in the Letters of Paul*, (New Haven: Yale University Press, 1989) that Paul's hermeneutical reading strategy construes scripture as a grand narrative of election and promise.

14. See my discussion of these passages in *Echoes of Scripture in the Letters of Paul*, 54-57, 95-102.

15. J. L. Houlden, *Ethics and the New Testament* (New York: Oxford University Press, 1973); Jack T. Sanders, *Ethics in the New Testament: Change and Development* (Philadelphia: Fortress, 1975); Allen Verhey, *The Great Reversal: Ethics and the New Testament* (Grand Rapids: Eerdmans, 1984); Siegfried Schulz, *Neutestamentliche Ethik* (Zürich: TVZ 1987); Wolfgang Schrage, *The Ethics of the New Testament*, trans. David E. Green (Philadelphia: Fortress, 1988); L. William Countryman, *Dirt, Greed, and Sex: Sexual Ethics in the New Testament and Their Implications for Today* (Philadelphia: Fortress, 1988); Eduard Lohse, Theological Ethics of the New Testament, trans. M. Eugene Boring (Minneapolis: Fortress, 1991); and Willi Marxsen, *New Testament Foundations for Christian Ethics*, trans. O. C. Dean, Jr. (Minneapolis: Fortress, 1993).

16. J. T. Sanders, 57.

17. Ibid., emphasis mine.

18. For a more ecclesiologically sensitive reading of Romans 12, see Marva J. Dawn, *The Hilarity of Community: Romans 12 and How to Be the Church* (Grand Rapids: Eerdmans, 1992).

19. J. T. Sanders, 65. (Cf. Gal. 6:10!) It should also be noted that Sanders then chastises Paul for being inconsistent in his specific moral teachings by appealing to "revelation from the Lord" rather than to the general moral principle of doing the good (66)!

20. Lohse, 105-13.

21. Rudolf Bultmann, *Theology of the New Testament*, Vol 1., trans. K. Grobel (New York: Charles Scribner's Sons, 1951), 185-352.

22. One working title for this essay was "The Apostle Paul and the Individualistic Hermeneutic of the West," but in the end I opted for a more constructively descriptive—and less derivative—title.

23. Victor P. Furnish, *Theology and Ethics in Paul* (Nashville: Abingdon, 1968), 203, emphasis his.

24. Ibid., 233, emphasis his.

25. Ibid., 212-24, quotation from p. 213.

26. Banks, *Paul's Idea of Community*, see n. 4 above; T. J. Deidun, *New Covenant Morality* in Paul, AnBib 89 (Rome: Biblical Institute, 1981); and J. Paul Sampley, *Walking between the Times: Paul's Moral Reasoning* (Minneapolis: Fortress, 1991).

27. It is tempting to speculate about the reasons for the relative neglect of this book. At-least three factors come to mind: 1) The book is written for a popular audience rather than as a scholarly monograph; 2) At the time of the book's publication, Banks was teaching in Australia rather than in Europe or America; 3) Perhaps most importantly, Banks' work came out just at the time when NT scholarship was newly engrossed in rhetorical criticism and in social-scientific study of the Pauline communities; thus, Banks' fundamentally *theological* study of Paul's *idea* of community fell among thorns, as it were.

28. Deidun, 45-50.

29. See now also N. T. Wright, *The Climax of the Covenant: Christ and the Law in Pauline Theology* (Minneapolis: Fortress, 1991).

30. Sampley, 37-43. See also pp. 60-62, 66-69.

31. In addition to the works mentioned here, see also the unpublished 1987 Yale dissertation by Sally Purvis, "Problems and Possibilities in Paul's Ethics of Community" (Ann Arbor: University Microfilms), some of whose content is summarized in Sally B. Purvis, *The Power of the Cross: Foundations for a Christian Feminist Ethic of Community* (Nashville: Abingdon, 1993). Walter Klaiber, *Rechtfertigung und Gemeinde: Eine Untersuchung zum paulinischen Kirchenverständnis,* FRLANT 127 (Göttingen: Vandenhoeck & Ruprecht, 1982), explores the relation of Paul's ecclesiology to his doctrine of justification, but deals only tangentially with ethics (e.g., pp 249-55).

32. Gerd Theissen, *The Social Setting of Pauline Christianity: Essays on Corinth* (Philadelphia: Fortress, 1982); Meeks, *The First Urban Christians,* see n. 3 above.

33. Meeks, *The First Urban Christians,* 74- 110.

34. Hans Dieter Betz, *Galatians: A Commentary on Paul's Letter to the Churches of Galatia,* Hermeneia (Philadelphia: Fortress, 1979), 292.

35. On this passage see Hays, "Christology and Ethics in Galatians: The Law of Christ."

36. Ernst Käsemann—the inveterate champion of the thesis that "Christology is the permanent measure of all ecclesiology"—would no doubt be scandalized by such an affirmation and fulminate against it. See Ernst Käsemann, "Paul and Early Catholicism," trans. Wilfred F. Bunge, in *New Testament Questions of Today* (Philadelphia: Fortress, 1969), 258.

37. Margaret M. Mitchell, *Paul and the Rhetoric of Reconciliation: An Exegetical Investigation of the Language and Composition of 1 Corinthians* (Louisville: Westminster/John Knox, 1992), 17, has demonstrated conclusively by means of rhetorical analysis that "1 Corinthians is a unified letter which throughout urges the course of unity on the divided Corinthian church."

38. A similar hermeneutical shift occurred in the Qumran writings: the community of the Covenanters was seen as replacing the corrupt temple in Jerusalem. See Bertil Gärtner, *The Temple and the Community in Qumran and the New Testament,* SNTSMS 1 (Cambridge: Cambridge University Press, 1965) .

39. Theissen, 125-29.

40. Paul does not actually use the term "strong" in 1 Cor 8; however, the term does appear in his discussion of a very similar problem in Rom 14: 1-15:6. See also the rhetorically freighted remark of 1 Cor 1:27: "God has chosen the foolish things of the world to shame the wise, and the weak things of the world to shame the strong."

41. See Dale Martin, *Slavery as Salvation: A Metaphor of Slavery in Pauline Christianity* (New Haven: Yale University Press, 1990), 86-116, on the *topos* of the "enslaved leader."

42. *Pace* Peter J. Tomson, *Paul and the Jewish Law: Halakha in the Letters of the Apostle to the Gentiles,* Compendium Rerum Iudaicarum ad Novum Testamentum, Section III, Vol. 1 (Assen/Maastricht: Van Gorcum and Minneapolis: Fortress, 1990).

43. P. 97. At the time of writing *Echoes of Scripture in the Letters of Paul,* I noted only the parallel in Deut 17:7, but the topic of Deut 22:13-30 is much more clearly related to the issue that Paul is addressing in Corinth. Note especially the ending of the section in Deut 22:30: "A man shall not marry his father's wife, thereby violating his father's rights."

THE CHURCH IN THE NEW TESTAMENT, SERVANT AND VICTORIOUS

FRANÇOIS BOVON

INTRODUCTION

The way the churches understand themselves today varies considerably from one theologian to another, from one pastor to another, and from one church member to another. Some think that a church that does not bring people to conversion cannot be the church of Jesus Christ. Others think of the church in connection with a particular confessional tradition and its history. A defense of the church understood that way is at the same time an apology for a tongue and for a nation. Still others neglect the structures and their inevitable power to embed the church into the radical gospel: if Christians forget the social trend of the good news and omit giving priority to the needs of the poor, they do not belong to the true church. Finally many church leaders consider their task to be the edification of the congregation: to preserve what exists, to help members in their struggles, and to build a lively congregation. To the impressive multiplicity of emphases we have to add a not less formidable doctrinal diversity in numerous Christian denominations. Churches with similar goals may diverge widely in their understanding of Christ or in their conception of the sacraments.

In a famous paper delivered first in English in 1955 and published in Canada, Rudolf Bultmann proposed a new understanding of the NT church.[1] Instead of a harmonious origin, he proposed a polemical development. He considered four phases in the self understanding of the primitive church. First, the early church thought of herself as the holy congregation of the last time. In this stage the Christians are still Jews; no break with Judaism has yet occurred. Second, the incorporation of Gentiles into the church expressed a first transformation. The church becomes a holy community gathering Jews and Gentiles in its unity. Because it is a body, what counts is no longer the eschatology, but the anticipation through the Holy Spirit of the kingdom in the reality of the church. Third, a second transformation occurred, according to Bultmann, when the people of God were no longer constituted by history (the event of Christ) but by the sacrament. Before this transformation the church was the "People of God"; with it she becomes now the "Body of Christ." As the many members have different duties in a single body, the numerous Christians have to be organized into a single institution. The ministry is established and a hierarchy emerges. The future of the individual soul takes over the collective eschatology. The delay of the parousia plays a large role in this evolution. The church becomes an institution of salvation, and the minister becomes a priest. Fourth, in the last stage, according to Bultmann, the Christian faith became a new religion and the church a worldwide institution (the "third race" beside Jews and Gentiles). Therefore it now becomes possible to write a history of the church as, for example, in the canonical Acts of the Apostles.

Some years later, at an ecumenical meeting of the Commission for Faith and Order in Montreal (1963), Ernst Käsemann agreed with his teacher that there is no one single canonical and authoritative ecclesiology in the NT, but offered a different view of the origins of Christianity.[2] Instead of a historical linear evolution, he proposed a sociological picture. Diversity is not successive, but contemporaneous. The unity of the church (which was the goal of the Montreal gathering and is still the objective of the World Council of Churches) has not been a historical reality, but an imperative objective for which it was necessary to fight. What was concrete and real in the first century were tensions, struggles, and divisions among Christians. This reality was created by different religious backgrounds, social contexts, and personal realities. But this plurality of church experiences did not eliminate a strong common belief. After all, these fighting congregations regarded themselves as Christian, meaning that they all descended from the same Jesus and they all believed that he was the Messiah, resurrected from the dead by God his father.

I consider myself to be in the line of Ernst Käsemann with regard to ecclesiology. I believe that in the beginning there were several different Christian groups: the circle of the twelve,[3] the so-called Hellenists,[4] the members of Jesus' family including James the brother of the Lord, the Johannine congregation under the patronage of the mysterious beloved disciple, and the radical itinerant missionaries and prophets.[5] These groups all had reasons to disagree because of their divergent roots in Judaism, because of their conflicting social worlds (urban versus rural, wealth versus poverty, education versus ignorance, freedom versus slavery). At the same time these groups shared a common spiritual treasury. This common faith, grounded in the love of God, nevertheless gave rise to divisions and struggles. The paradox is a true paradox and not a softened contradiction. It will be my intention in these pages to respect first the *differences*, but to also see that in the reactions of the various groups as well as in their given reality, there were common Christian elements which can be shared in a true church experience. In a world of divisions, oppression, and hate, different groups and various individual believers could constitute—because of their faith, hope, and love, because of God's will, Christ's intercession, and the Holy Spirit's presence—the visible and invisible, the holy and the sinful, the present and the eschatological church, full of memory and hope, of sharp awareness of the presence of evil as well as knowledge of God, "the one apostolic and universal church."

THE COMMON FAITH

For this part I am dependent on what I have learned as a student from teachers like Oscar Cullmann, Franz J. Leenhardt, and Eduard Schweizer, and from Roman Catholic exegetes such as Lucien Cerfaux and Rudolf Schnackenburg.[6] Because of the intellectual influence of the Roman Catholic tradition in France, it is logical that the question of ecclesiology has been widely discussed among French speaking exegetes. The spirit of that time also contributed to the discussion; it was the time of Vatican II and of the ecumenical movement. A description of the common faith of the early church should include at least four elements.

1. Some Jews, touched by Jesus' teaching, came to believe after his capital punish-

ment that he had been vindicated by God. Resurrected and exalted, Jesus has, according to them, been designated as the Messiah of Israel and the Son of God. A new relation to him emerged, which they called "faith." Those believers were the true remnant of the people of God, the calling of the lost sheep of Israel. They were dependent on God's call and on Christ's mediation. The emphasis was on unity, cohesion, common belief, and communion in love (what Luke expresses retrospectively in Acts 2:46). Several terms were used by the Christians themselves to designate what they had in common: "disciples" (Acts 6:2); "the holy ones" (Acts 9:3); the "brothers" (Acts 10:23); the "elected" (Luke 18:7 and Mark 13:20); and later the "Christians" (Acts 11:28 and 1 Pet 4:16). This last name had not been a self-designation, but was given by non-Christians in Antioch to designate the new religious movement.[7] But the most important name which was chosen was the Greek word *ekklēsia.* This term was convenient because it was neglected by the Jews who preferred the word *synagōge,* "synagogue," and it was used by the Greeks as a political term. (It meant the political assembly of the citizens of a polis, of a city). So the Christians avoided any syncretistic connotation: religious associations in Greece were called religious guilds, clubs, or confraternities, but not churches.[8]

In the word *ekklēsia,* as well as in its Hebrew and Aramaic equivalents, the "calling" *(kaleō)* is the main meaning. The church feels herself called by God's initiative and God's power; she understands herself to be brought together and established as a unity. A divine and invisible force unifies and founds the church in spite of material distances and visible differences. Do not forget in the term *ekklēsia* is the preposition *ek,* "out of." To be a church means to come "out of" some—material and spiritual—place in the world. This term *ekklēsia,* used normally in the singular,[9] is not easy to translate. If you translate it as "community," you miss the universality of the one church. If you choose to translate it as "church," you are in danger of projecting into first century Christianity legal and institutional categories which are absent at this early stage.

2. There is an early Christian theological structure which helps us to give a second characteristic to the NT church. Besides the Christ event there is the apostolic responsibility. Using Paul's terminology, besides the "reconciliation" in Christ, there is and must be the "service of reconciliation."[10] The early Christians not only believed in what God had done reconciling the world through Christ, but they immediately shared this religious knowledge with others through preaching and witness in words and deeds. The centripetal force (which is acknowledged in the very word *ekklēsia)* is balanced by the centrifugal missionary activity. The oldest ministry was called "the apostolate."[11] As you know, etymologically, an apostle is a witness of Christ who "is sent" by his Lord to testify of the historical and suprahistorical truth. There is a similarity, an analogy between the life of the church and the life of its Lord: Jesus had been sent by God, the apostles in turn were sent by the Lord; Jesus had tried to bring Israel to repentance, the first Christians tried to bring first Jews then Gentiles through Jesus back to God the Creator and Redeemer; Jesus had given witness by words and deeds, the disciples preached and gave concrete signs of God's love for the world; Jesus refused to compromise and died as a victim of human reluctance; the church also has to suffer opposition and repulsion.[12]

3. Jesus preached the imminent coming of the kingdom. This apocalyptic atmosphere[13] remained determinant for the early Christians. The resurrection of Christ—resurrection meant the beginning of the last days—supported and confirmed this eschatological understanding of the present situation and of the nature of the church. Like the people who preserved the Dead Seas Scrolls,[14] the early Christians understood their existence as eschatological. They gave to Christ the Lord the title *prōtotokos,* "first born" of the new creation,[15] which infers that others will be taken into the procession of the new born

of the redemption. They interpreted the historical event of Good Friday and Easter in a typological way as the fulfillment of the first Exodus, the eschatological antitype of the protological type. The death of Jesus, particularly shocking at first glance, can be seen not as a misfortune, but as the sacrifice and sealing of the new covenant. The ritual as well actualizes this event and expresses the covenant. Baptism is seen as individual redemption. Eucharist is seen as the collective link with God and the communion of the Christians together. Finally, the coming of the Holy Spirit, first as a reality perceived, then as a reflection over that experience, confirms the eschatological dimension of the church and confronts her with the new image of God: Father, Son, and Spirit.

4. The gathering of the early Christians was at the same time a pleasure and a duty, a material reunion, when possible, and a spiritual convention in any case. They ate together and shared their resources: no poor should remain in need, which was already an ideal of the old Israel.[16] Money can be a demonic reality, but it can also be a benediction, a spiritual power. They prayed together. As long as possible they went to the synagogue to pray and share the word of God, but they came together for meetings at Easter and during the night from Saturday to Sunday, perhaps twice, once Saturday night and then on Sunday morning, the evening with the death of Jesus in mind, the morning with his resurrection on the heart. Their common prayer is first a eulogy, a benediction, a thanksgiving for the Creator of life who is also the Redeemer, the Father of Jesus, the beloved Son who has been sent for us. But prayer also has other dimensions such as petition and intercession. Together these people shared information (a factor NT scholars tend to forget) about one another and from congregation to congregation.[17] The *communio sanctorum* is not an empty expression. Baptism introduces new converts to the people of God: Christians are now sealed with the Spirit, consecrated by God, put into Christ's possession and introduced and incorporated into the church. The eucharist expresses the unity of the new congregation's unity in faith and in mutual love and in expectations of victory over death. Like the idealized image of Israel in the desert where it was dependent on God only, the Christians are "holy," the "saints," devoted to God, separated from Egypt, from the world.[18] This characteristic of the church, her holiness, is an ecclesiological category, and a cultic category, but also an ethical one. As the "saints," the Christian congregations shine in the night of this world, giving a good witness, attracting the attention of "those from outside."[19]

THREE EARLY CHRISTIAN CHURCHES

1. The Church of Q

A lot of discussion has taken place over the so-called source of the logia, the Q document.[20] It is my opinion that this document did exist and was used by both Matthew and Luke. It was a collection of Jesus' words which were collectcd by anonymous Christians, who should be identified neither with the group of the twelve nor with the Hellenists. Those who carried these words were radical Christians, trying to apply literally Jesus' requirements, itinerant missionaries with apocalyptic expectations, who had left behind them their families and their jobs, "everything." They tried to "follow" Jesus to "confess" his Lordship, to "suffer" for his name, etc. They may have walked in Galilee, then in Syria, speaking Aramaic, then Greek. They were Jews, but their acknowledgment of Jesus as the Son of Man brought them into conflict with the Pharisees and their radical evangelism with the Zealots. They may have been still observant of the Mosaic Law and consequently responsible for a kind of ritual falling back from Jesus' freedom into Jewish obedience. But they were Christians as is shown by their interest in Jesus, not only as a wise man or an apocalyptic visionary, but also, as God's only Son and expected Son of Man. Their theology was marked by one Jewish tradition, which originated in the deuteronomistic historiography. They believed that Israel constantly resisted God and that only a few authentic prophets would be faithful and that these prophets would be persecuted as many others before them—remember the understanding in Q of Jerusalem as the city that kills the prophets (Matt 23:37; Luke 13:34). Several of Jesus' sentences which they have transmitted help us to comprehend their understanding of God's people, their "ecclesiology:" the words on following (Matt 8:19-22 paralleled in Luke 9:57-60), the teaching on mission (Matt 10 paralleled in Luke 9-10), the Lord's prayer (Matt 6:9-13 paralleled in Luke 11: 1-4), the attack on the Pharisees (Matt 23 paralleled in Luke 11), and the so-called Johannine logia (Matt 11: 25-27 paralleled in Luke 10:21-22).

They were pleased to remember Jesus' prayer, "I thank you, Father, Lord of heaven and earth, because you have hidden these things from the wise and the intelligent and have revealed them to infants; yes, Father, for such was your gracious will," (Luke 10:21). In this single verse a full theology and a peculiar ecclesiology are beginning to take root:[21] a discovery of God as Creator ("Lord of heaven and earth"), but also, and first of all, as Redeemer (as "Father" with a "gracious will"). The Q community believes that Jesus has been the mediator between that God and themselves: "All things have been handed over to me by my Father; and no one knows who the Son is except the Father, or who the Father is except the Son and anyone to whom the Son chooses to reveal him." But particularly important for our topic is the way the Christian community, the church, is described here. First the church is presented in a polemical way. The sentence expresses first what she is not. She is not "wise," and she is not "intelligent." The church is not constituted from below by human resources like wisdom or intelligence. She is created from above by God himself. The Q community was not hostile to wisdom, but refused any human quest to obtain divine knowledge. Revelation that comes from grace is the only source of faith and wisdom. The Q congregation fought against the religious and intellectual power of the Jewish leaders—Sadducees, Pharisees or Essenes, who were sure of the validity of their theology. The Q congregation was also "sure and confident," but her strength was in her weakness, her intelligence was in her humility, and her maturity was in her childhood. "Infants" (*nēpioi*) was her ecclesiological title.[22] There is in the synoptic tradition an enhanced valuation of the child which is exceptional in the antique world. This attention to children is embedded in the teaching of the historical Jesus, but the Q congregation was keen to claim this heritage for herself. They were children of God who have received, better than a science, a revelation (you "have revealed them to infants," Luke 10:22). In their view Jesus' teaching was the revelation of God.

2. *The Church of the Book of Revelation*

With the book of Revelation[23] we leave Christianity in Syria and find another one, a Johannine one, in Asia. The Jewish War brought Jews and Christians from Palestine to Asia. The Johannine group formerly in Samaria was scattered and some members settled down in Ephesus. It is probable that two distinct Christian congregations existed in Ephesus at the dawn of the first century C.E., a Pauline one and a Johannine one. The time may be the end of Domitian's reign about 93-96 C.E. To enter the world of these Christians we can read the beginning of the book. Verses 1-3 of chapter 1 express the ambition and the authority of the author. He is sure to have received a revelation (like the "infants" of Q) from Jesus Christ who is (like in Q) the mediator:" "The revelation of Jesus Christ, which God gave him." The author believed himself to be an authorized and inspired prophet. The function of a prophet after the apostles was decisive in this kind of community as in the congregation of the Hellenists (cf. Acts 13:1-3) and in the congregations of the Pauline churches (cf. 1 Cor 12:28). He believed he was the servant of Jesus, God's mediator. His responsibility was to bring the revelation to the congregations. (According to the NT structure I have mentioned, beside the divine event comes the revelation; a human witness is needed, here John's witness, *marturia*). The divine revelation is not uniform in the NT: at times it is a revelation about the immediate future ("the time is close," Rev 1:3); elsewhere it is related to the immediate past ("these things," Luke 10:21, which are realized by Jesus himself).

The prophet has the responsibility, not just to be secretly pleased with himself, but to express in human words what has been disclosed to him. In so doing the prophet is at the same time weak (compared with powerful human leaders: Jewish scholars in Luke 10:21 or Roman Emperors in Revelation) and triumphant (in that he has received God's message, God's wisdom, and God's revelation).

This religious strength appears in the letter which follows. This epistle—actually the whole book of Revelation (Rev 1:4-22:21)—is the framework in which he will bring the divine revelation. He inserted into this framework the letters to the seven churches (Rev 2-3, where we have exceptionally the plural). The dialectic between the singular and plural corresponds to the interaction between the divine unity and the human diversity. In an archaic form John—such is the name of the prophet (cf. Rev 1:1 and 1:9)—first greeted the addressees. His extension of the grace of God in 1 :4 is made according to the Jewish understanding of Exod 3: 14. The present God ("who is") is the same as the God of the holy past ("who was") and of the coming future ("who shall come"). This grace comes also from the Spirit. Strangely enough the Spirit is seen in its richness and is identified with the angels who are at God's court ("the seven spirits, which are in front of his throne," Rev 1:4). Finally, the grace comes from Jesus Christ; the trinitarian order Father—Son—Spirit is not yet established. The prophet has to explain the nature and the function of his Christ by saying that Christ is the witness, the faithful one, and the firstborn from the dead. He reminds his readers of the three steps of Jesus' life: the ministry through the word, the passion, and the resurrection. Saying that Christ loves us (note the present) and that he has delivered us, John affirms that the future cannot threaten the soteriological fact. On the contrary, the future of the church can only be a participation in the Lamb's triumph. As he is himself the winner, his people are not only liberated from the sinful past, but are also established in the present and for the future as heirs of God's kingdom and priests of his spiritual temple. This holy past and this divine present can only merge into an eschatological, imminent, future. According to 1:3b the received revelation means that the time is short, because the Winner comes to celebrate his victory. His troops will experience triumph, but his adversaries will encounter defeat (v. 7b).

This was the address and the greeting of the long letter which is the book of Revelation.Then comes the narrative, the story explaining and justifying how, when, and where John received this divine message: "I, John, your brother who share with you in Jesus the persecution and the kingdom and the patient endurance, was on the island called Patmos because of the word of God and the testimony of Jesus" (1:9). Historically this means that the prophet had been put on trial by a Roman court for spreading religious propaganda and condemned to deportation and slave labor. But through his faith John learned how to look at history with God's eye. This is a case of prophecy: the deportation and slave labor are real, but there is space for Sunday prayer, religious experience, and contact with God through the Spirit (1:10). What he experienced in Patmos was not the privilege of an exquisite believer, but the destiny of each Christian, the destiny of the church in the society: suffering and winning, servanthood and triumph. John did not use his proximity with Christ and his prophetic ministry to establish a hierarchical authority. As prophet he did not become the father of the Asian churches, but remained a brother. He was so little an exception that he called himself a companion, someone literally "who is a companion sharing with you" (note the redundancy *sug—koinōnos*). What he shares is exactly the topic of this paper; the *thlipsis*, the "tribulation," the "suffering," and the *basileia*, the "kingdom," the "triumph."

This tension between humility (humiliation) and glory (kingship) is the human condition, the present destiny of the church. It is also an ethical tension, where Christ's will must be in harmony with the children's decisions. The communion between John and the Asian churches is a communion of *hypomonē*, a word well translated by "patient endurance." There is a passive side in *hypomonē*, what you suffer from someone else, and an active side, the resistance or endurance you offer with all your force.

In this autobiographical presentation of John, we also have a theological definition of the church according to the book of Revelation: servant on one side, bride on the other; suffering in the world, but promised the imminent triumph of the Lamb. In confrontation with the world and its powers the church aims for the welfare and the future salvation of the whole world.

3. *The Pauline Church*

The usual way to deal with Pauline ecclesiology is to turn to the Pastoral Epistles or to the Epistles to the Ephesians and to the Colossians. That is to appeal to later developments, to institutional or ideological solutions given in a time when the church had to be stabilized in order to survive. The *notae ecclesiae*, the marks of the church, as they appear in the main authentic epistles are often neglected or distorted. And when the genuine letters are under scrutiny,1 Corinthians falls normally under the spotlight.[24] I propose to consider here primarily the Epistle to the Romans. For even if the word *ekklēsia*, "church," does not occur in this letter, its author manifests a constant ecclesiological care.[25] I concentrate our attention on the famous ending of chapter 8, verses 31b-39: "If God is for us, who is against us?. . . For I am convinced that neither death, nor life, nor angels, nor rulers, nor things present, nor things to come, nor powers, nor height, nor depth, nor anything else in all creation, will be able to separate us from the love of God in Christ Jesus our Lord." Of great interest here is the use of "us," for the first person plural pronoun represents the whole company of the believers, the glorious Christian "church."

But the reader must be careful. When the apostle wrote this epistle from Corinth in the year 56 or 57, he was far from being victorious. On the contrary, he had three main sources of anxiety.[26] First, in Corinth, where he was staying, he was not sure that the dangerous enthusiasm he tried to eradicate some time earlier would not reemerge. In order to prevent such a risk he wrote chapters 14-15 on the relation between the so-called "strong" and "weak." Second, he was not sure what would happen in Jerusalem where his path would lead him soon. Paul was taking to the "saints" of the Jewish capital the collection for which he accepted organizational responsibility at the closing session of the famous Jerusalem conference (in approximately 48, cf. Gal 2:10). As he knew of judaizing opposition against his understanding of Christian freedom, he feared that the Jerusalem mother church would refuse the gift of the Gentile Christian congregations of the diaspora. Behind this tension between two wings of the Christian movement, he felt the broader problematic of the connections between Judaism, the genuine olive tree, and Christianity, the wild olive tree. The apostle wrote chapters 9-11 in order to clarify his own position on the relation between Israel and the church. By so doing he hoped to help the Roman congregation gain a sound understanding of this relation. Third, Paul kept to his goal of reaching Rome after stopping in Jerusalem and before going to Spain (Rom15:22-29). What was the situation of the Roman congregation? Was her internal life firmly harmonious in its relations between Christians of Jewish and Christians of Gentile origins? The apostle gave his attention first to this question and tried in chapters 1-8 to give a clear theological teaching on this interrelation between Jews and Gentiles within the people of God. But he did not develop his thought without fear.

If Paul speaks often of "us," of the "Christians," in Rom 8:31b-39, in spite of the triumphant tone of his voice, he does not have in mind a victorious church without problems, nor a congregation abundant in charity, well-rooted in the faith and sealed in unity. What makes this "us" "far more than conquerors" (Rom 8:37) is not the quality of church administration, nor the unity of doctrine, nor the splendor of liturgy, nor the success of missionary campaigns, nor the authenticity of spiritual experiences, but only, as the text states it: the one God who loves us. Therefore "in all these things we are more than conquerors through him who loved us" (Rom 8:37).

In Rom 8:18-28 Paul has shown that Christians share with the rest of humanity its suffering and its finitude. They complain and they groan, as everybody, because, if they are to be saved, it is still in hope (Rom 8:24). With this observation, the apostle seems to have reached an end: "What then are we to say about these things" (Rom 8:31). But he was not pleased to conclude merely with this recording of a global frustration, the misery of this world and the suffering of the church. He was also keen to mention a difference between the present situation of the world and that of the church. He liked to recall what he had said at 8:1: "There is therefore now no condemnation for those who are in Christ Jesus." So he reminded his Roman readers that the Christians already belong to the new world, to the new creation. And this eschatological privilege, the old world, the old society, cannot bear without polemical reaction.

Here is the paradox of Rom 8:31-39. Nowhere else does Paul mention more diligently the victory of the Christian believers, their justification, and their glorification. But nowhere else either is the opposition of the world to the true church mentioned more boldly. If the tension between this triumph and this defeat of the church, of the "us," can be finally suppressed, it is because the origin of the church's victory does not lie in human power, but is only possible through God's action. Left alone, the church, like any human institution, could only waste away and finally perish. Only Christ's victory under God's leadership has overcome the sin, the finitude and the death.[27]

Conclusion

There are marks of the church I have not underlined sufficiently, especially preaching and the sacraments. There are ecclesiological themes I have only mentioned, notably the divine calling and the gathering of God's people after the Easter victory, the gift of the Holy Spirit and the new life it makes possible, the organization and the growth of Christ's body, and the truly Christian actions inside and outside the organized church. There are other Christian groups I have not described, starting with the most venerable one, the church of the twelve in Jerusalem. But I have tried to show that in spite of sociological, ideological, and cultural discrepancies the churches of the first century, as far as we can reach them through a critical exegesis of the NT, all have a common specificity which designates them as Christians. They possess in Christ a richness, a power, and a wisdom that nobody can steal from them because it is not from this world, but begins already to transform this world. Certainly, distinct from the others, "aside," the Christians will soon suffer from contempt, then from persecution. Rom 8:36 summarizes well what I wanted to bring into light: "As it is written, 'For your sake we are being killed all day long; we are accounted as sheep to be slaughtered." Because God let us share in his Kingdom, because we have received a divine strength, we can fulfill a stewardship and take over responsibilities which will lead us into trouble and pains. Our existence as church members will therefore conform to Christ's destiny.

There is a christomorphy in the church's life. This christomorphy is grounded in the fact that the Christians have been incorporated into the body of Christ. (Cf. 1 Cor 6:15-17; 12:12-31; and Rom 12:4-5). Just as they have received Christ in themselves, they bear him.[28] They have clothed themselves with him (Gal 3:27). Through Christ, the death of Christians, as well as their life, can receive a positive meaning. The theological structure I have tried to highlight with its two poles, glory and service, is embedded in the dialectic (more than the succession) of Good Friday and Easter. In different words, it is present in the three traditions we have discussed. In Paul, it is the tension between the present justification and the present tribulation. In the Book of Revelation, it is the reign of the believers who cannot escape the persecution of the beasts. For the Q congregation, it is God's revelation given to vulnerable infants. Such an ecclesiology in its strength and weakness can be found in other parts of the NT, from Luke to 1 Peter. It was a common conviction of all the first Christians, from Peter to Timothy, from Mary to Lydia.[29]

NOTES

1. Rudolf Bultmann, "The Transformation of the Idea of the Church in the History of Early Christianity," *Canadian Journal of Theology*, 1 (1955), 73-81.

2. "Unité et diversité dans l'ecclésiologie du Nouveau Testament," *Études Théologiques et Religieuses*, 48 (1966), 253-258. See also "The Canon of the New Testament and the Unity of the Church," *Essays on New Testament Themes*, trans. W. J. Montague, SBT 41 (Napierville, IL: Allenson, 1964), 95-101.

3. Under the leadership of Peter.

4. Under the leadership of the seven, particularly Stephen and Philip, and later of Paul.

5. There are several reconstructions of the early churches. Among them see François Vouga, *A l'aube du christianisme, une surprenante diversité* (Aubonne, Switzerland: Le Moulin, 1986).

6. Cf. Oscar Cullmann, La foi et le culte de L'Église primitive, Bibliothèque théologique (Neuchâtel: Delachaux & Niestlé, 1963); Franz J. Leenhardt, L'Église: Questions aux protestants et aux catholiques, Lieux theologiques 1 (Genève: Labor et Fides, 1978); Eduard Schweizer, *Church Order in the New Testament*, SBT 32, trans. Frank Clarke (London: SCM, 1961); Lucien Cerfaux, *The Church in the Theology of Saint Paul*, trans. Geoffrey Webb and Adrian Walker (New York: Herder & Herder, 1959); Rudolph Schnackenburg, *The Church in the New Testament*, trans. W. J. O'Hara (New York: Herder & Herder, 1965).

7. Cf. François Bovon, *Luke the Theologian: Thirty-Three Years of Research (1950-1983)*, Princeton Theological Monograph Series 12 (Allison Park, PA: Pickwick, 1987), 320-321.

8. Cf. Karl-Ludwig Schmidt, "*Kaleō*," TDNT, III, 487-536; and Wayne A. Meeks, *The First Urban Christians: The Social World of the Apostle Paul* (New Haven: Yale University Press, 1983), 74.

9. Cf. 1 Cor 1:2 for example: "The church of God which is in Corinth...."

10. 2 Cor 5:18-21. Cf. François Bovon, *L'Évangile et l'Apôtre; Le Christ inséparable de ses témoins* (Aubonne, Switzerland: Le Moulin, 1993).

11. Cf. Karl Heinrich Rengstorf, "*apostellō* ," TDNT, I, 398-447.

12. Cf. John 15:18.

13. The present tendency in the United States to replace this apocalyptic orientation with a wisdom perspective does not seem correct to me. It is perhaps dependent more on the present situation of Christianity than on the original meaning of the texts of the NT.

14. The congregation believed themselves to be the true remnant of Israel and to be in the last days. Cf. Gal 6: 16.

15. Cf. Heb 1:8 and Col 1:15 and 18.

16. Cf. Acts 4:34 which is dependent on Deut 15:4.

17. Cf. François Bovon, "L'origine des récits concernant les apôtres," *Revue de theologie et de philosophie*, 3rd ser., 1 (1967), 345-350.

18. The typology of the Exodus is used effectively in preaching at Easter, as can be seen in the patristic treatises. See, for example, *The Homily "On the Passover"* by Melito of Sardis.

19. Cf. Matt 5:14-16 and Phil 2:15.

20. Cf. John Kloppenborg, *The Formation of Q: Trajectories in Ancient Wisdom Collections*, Studies in Antiquity and Christianity (Philadelphia: Fortress Press, 1987).

21. For a bibliography and a full explanation, cf. the forthcoming second volume of my commentary on Luke's gospel.

22. Etymologically the word *nēpios*, like *infans* in Latin, means a child which cannot yet-speak. On this word cf. Simon Legasse, *Jésus et l'enfant. "Enfants," "petits" et "simples" dans la tradition synoptique*, Études bibliques (Paris: Gabalda, 1969).

23. On Revelation, cf. Pierre Prigent, *L'Apocalypse de saint Jean*, 2d ed, Commentaire du Nouveau Testament, 2e série, 14 (Genève: Labor et Fides, 1988).

24. There are nevertheless good studies on Paul's ecclesiology. Cf. for example, Josef-Hainz, *Ekklesia: Strukturen paulinischer Gemeinde-Theologie und Gemeinde-Ordnung*, Biblische Untersuchungen 9 (Regensburg: Pustet, 1972); and Gosnell L. O. R. Yorke, *The Church as the Body of Christ in the Pauline Corpus: A Re-examination* (Lanham, MD: University Press of America, 1991).

25. In his introduction to his commentary on Romans, Franz J. Leenhardt has insisted on this point. See *The Epistle to the Romans: A Commentary*, trans. Harold Knight (Cleveland: World Publishing Company, 1961), 13-23.

26. Cf. Günther Bornkamm, "Der Römerbrief als Testament des Paulus," *Geschichte und Glaube, zweiter Teil, Gesammelte Aufsätze*, Beitrage zur evangelische Theologie 53 (München: Kaiser, 1971), IV, 120-133.

27. On Rom 8:31-39, cf. Ernst Käsemann, *Commentary on Romans*, trans. Geoffrey W. Bromiley (Grand Rapids: Eerdmans, 1980), 245-252.

28. The adjective *christophoros* ("Christ-bearing") is used first by Ignatius of Antioch, Ephesians 9.2; then it is applied to martyrs in a letter written by Phileas of Thmuis quoted by Eusebius of Caesarea, *Historia ecclesiastica* VIII.10.3.

29. After completion of this paper, I received Eduard Schweizer's review (*Theologische Literaturzeitung*, 119, 1994, 655-658) of Jürgen Roloff, *Die Kirche im Neuen Testament*, Grundrisse zum Neuen Testament 10 (Göttingen: Vandenhoeck & Ruprecht, 1993.)

RESPONSE

WALTER L. LIEFELD

Bovon's paper, like the New Testament churches it surveys, is rich in both its diversity and its unity. I appreciated its balanced approach between the common faith and the individuality of the early churches, a balance that we sometimes lose. The initial observations on the contemporary church are incisive and fair. I would like to return to this shortly. I agree with Bovon's choice of Käsemann's sociological view of ecclesiastical diversity over Bultmann's, that is, contemporaneous rather than linear, evolutionary diversity. One aspect of this is the issue of forms of ministry within the various ecclesiastical structures. This recalls the earlier perspectives of von Campenhausen, Käsemann and others who saw opposing forms of ministry in the so-called charismatic churches represented by Corinth and in the organized ministry of the Pastorals. This both undervalued the presence of organization in Corinthians (e.g., the lists of apostolic, prophetic, etc. ministries) and the spiritual endowments and prophetic pronouncements accompanying the laying on of hands in the Pastorals (1 Tim 4:14; 2 Tim 1:6). Among those who have addressed this matter even handedly is R. K. Y. Fung, in a series of articles on ministry in *The Evangelical Quarterly*. See especially "Charismatic versus Organized Ministry? An Examination of an Alleged Antithesis" (52, 1980, 195-214) and "Ministry, Community and Spiritual Gifts" (56, 1984, 3-20). H. C. Kee showed in a 1992 article that while there is diversity of leadership modes between the Synoptic, Johannine and Pauline literature, there is no strong difference.

Also in the paper before us, I appreciated the reference to *ekklēsia* and the idea of calling. Personally (and this is only a small point) I prefer not even to cite the etymological function of the *ek* prefix because it was misused by some who left the main line denominations in the 1930's and 40's to justify their coming "out" of those bodies. (Right or wrong, there were better reasons.) In the Greek city-state democratic systems, the *ekklēsia* was the body that came out from the surrounding areas for the purpose of being *together*. Of far more importance is the significance of the term *ekklēsia*, which Bovon emphasizes. The idea of callIng is of great importance. It is noteworthy that even the divided Corinthian church was addressed several times at the outset of 1 Corinthians as called by God.

Further unifying factors that could have been developed are, of course, the table of the Lord and the relation of the church to the kingdom, but those were choices that had to be made to keep the paper within limits. It is a matter for continual regret that such matters, which should have united the church, became a cause for division over the church's history.

Of the three portraits Bovon sketched, the Q community, the Pauline and the Johannine, I most enjoyed the last. This is in large measure because I had never thought that broadly, having, perhaps like others, mainly noted the churches of Revelation 2 and 3 rather than the shape of the church portrayed in the book as a whole. Regarding the "Q community," while I am open to the common supposition that Q was a document, I am reluctant to reconstruct a community of believers and their doctrines from it. With regard to the Pauline churches in Rome, Romans 9-11 and then 14-15 on the strong and the weak may well reflect sociological diversity, assuming the banishment of the Jewish believers under the edict of Claudius and the tensions that may well have developed on their return after a period of Gentile leadership in that church. It would also be interesting to note the tensions in Acts where in chapter fifteen there is both unity (the apostolic decree) and disunity (Paul and Barnabas).

I would like to add at this point some observations as a pastor, asking how we can apply such insights from the early church about unity and diversity, servanthood and victory, to the contemporary scene, espcially as regards those churches that are emerging in strength as we approach the year 2000.

We are used to the categories of (1) individual churches, "house churches" in the early period, (2) city wide or regional groups of churches (3) the "church universal" and sometimes (4) the church triumphant, beyond this life. Taking the first two categories into consideration, there was, as we have seen in Bovon's paper, an underlying commonality, a servant attitude and confidence of victory. Today the units of believers appear in quite different forms. Among these are:

a. Para church movements that have become quasi-church groups.
b. Personality dominated groups, often cultish even if orthodox, under a strict authority.
c. Mega-churches, many of which follow the "Willow Creek model" and stress outreach to unchurched "seekers."
d. Meta-churches, which may also be large, that have a deliberate agenda for change in order to adapt to the future, where there may be an equal emphasis on cell groups that function as mini-churches and a large gathering for "celebration."
e. Conglomerate churches that function with a full ministry and celebration of sacraments (or observance of ordinances), but operate in conjunction with a strong central leadership. Such an arrangement was pioneered in Atlanta with the slogan,"one church, many congregations."
f. Culturally homogenous churches. Some recent examples are those that are not necessarily ethnic, but comprise business and professional, often single, people in their 20's and 30's.
g. Restoration churches. In older examples, these seek to follow NT "patterns." Older examples included the Disciples of Christ and Plymouth Brethren. More recent is the desire to restore NT spiritual gifts. In addition to Pentecostal and charismatic groups there is the rapidly growing Vineyard movement
h. Metropolitan Community churches serve the gays and lesbians who desire to worship as Christians but feel, or are, excluded from other churches.

These categories are often due to the kind of origin they had, just as was the case in the early church. There were different apostles and other itinerent preachers, different cultures, ethnic differences and so on. This is to say nothing of major doctrinal differences. But there are also other, sometimes more subtle, differences.

Today churches are influenced by outside forces such as TV preachers, movements and various publications, e.g., Robert Schuler, James Dobson, feminist and anti-feminist opinions, *The Christian Century* and *Christianity Today.* Churches today are increasingly characterized by different styles in worship, especially in music. Bigbie of Cambridge has shown how many of these (and here we go back to the title of Bovon's paper) concentrate on a triumphalistic, Christus Victor theme, rather than the servanthood and suffering of Christ.

This symposium is concerned with the theological interpretation of scripture. I have extended this to apply to contemporary expressions of ecclesiology in some of the rapidly expanding American churches. But there is one glaring omission. The contemporary literature that feeds these churches is often devoid of biblical exegesis and theological reflection. David Wells examined a number of volumes of *Leadership* and was distressed at how little biblical content he found. See his book entitled *No Place for Truth or Whatever Happened to Evangelical Theology?* (Grand Rapids: Eerdmans, 1993), especially 106-115. I recently read an excellent, influential book on preparing the church for the future. I realized after finishing how little reference there was to scripture—two references to Job and one to the Psalms. Let it be said that this was not intended to be a theological work. My hope, however, is that as we plan for our churches today and tomorrow, we do so with full awareness of the trends, problems, diversity and common bonds of the early church, as evidenced in Bovon's paper, and that we apply such insights to the church of today, with all of its diversity and potential.

JESUS AND THE CHURCH
An Essay on Ecclesial Hermeneutics

CARL E. BRAATEN

INTRODUCTION: REVISITING AN OLD THEME

The quest of the historical Jesus has again become a major preoccupation of modern NT scholars. It originated as a project of the Enlightenment and continued to be carried on throughout the nineteenth century by the application of ever increasingly sophisticated methods of historical criticism. However, at the beginning of the twentieth century, dialectical and neo-orthodox theologians completely abandoned the quest as both historically impossible and theologically irrelevant. Furthermore, they could point to Albert Schweitzer's influential history of the movement in his monumental work, *The Quest of the Historical Jesus,*[1] as a kind of irrefutable obituary, even though Schweitzer himself believed that, though all previous scholars had failed for one reason or another, he himself had finally established the definitive truth about the real historical Jesus. At any rate, Paul Tillich credited Schweitzer, along with Martin Kähler, for having placed in question the entire Jesus-research program.

Tillich wrote: "Seen in the light of its basic intention, the attempt of historical criticism to find the empirical truth about Jesus of Nazareth was a failure. The historical Jesus, namely, the Jesus behind the symbols of his reception as the Christ, not only did not appear but receded farther and farther with every new step."[2] During the heydey of neo-orthodoxy systematic and dogmatic theologians were not really interested in the historical Jesus. Moreover, Rudolf Bultmann, speaking from the standpoint of critical scholarship, offered them no good reason why they should be interested. Bultmann stated: "We can, strictly speaking, know nothing of the personality of Jesus."[3] And that is no loss, because that would be to know Jesus only *kata sarka* and not *kata pneuma* (cf. 2 Cor 5:16). The mood of historical skepticism was pervasive and pronounced. Emil Brunner commented: "Even the bare fact of the existence of Christ as an historical person is not assured."[4]

Just when it seemed that systematic and dogmatic theology had successfully constructed their systems on purely apostolic, kerygmatic, and confessional foundations, Ernst Käsemann called for a renewal of the quest of the historical Jesus—and for theological reasons. The kerygma of the exalted Lord includes the life history of Jesus and would vanish into docetic idealism without it. It was a clear protest against his teacher Bultmann. Others of the "Old Marburgers" (Bultmannians) answered Käsemann's call—Gunther Bornkamm, Hans Conzelmann, and Ernst Fuchs. The New Quest proved to be significantly different from the Old Quest entombed by Schweitzer. It did not pretend to be primarily a historico-scientific project; it was motivated chiefly by the specific interest of faith in the gospel. As a theological program the scholars of the new quest were not in search "of supposed historical *bruta facta* but only...of the connection and tension between the preaching of Jesus and that of his community."[5]

Basically, the New Questers had no new methods or new texts that could solve the problem of the historical Jesus. They sought to anchor the kerygma of the church in the preaching, teaching, and activity of Jesus. Christian faith required it, otherwise it would dissolve into a kind of myth of a mystery religion. Gerhard Ebeling went on to write a comprehensive dogmatics on the basis of the theological perspective and historical findings of the new quest. Wolfhart Pannenberg agreed with the basic theological judgment of Käsemann and company that any attempt to construct christology without going back behind the apostolic kerygma to the historical Jesus is self-contradictory, because the central christological confession of the earliest Christian community is grounded in the activity and destiny of the man Jesus. Christology is the church's interpretation of Jesus of Nazareth, his life, ministry, death and resurrection. Pannenberg's turn to history and the historical approach constituted his decisive break with the prevailing Barthian and Bultmannian alternatives.

In this essay I am revisiting an old theme for me. After I passed my doctoral field examinations at Harvard University in 1957, I made an appointment to see Paul Tillich. For two years I had been wrangling with him on the Trinity and christology, and he knew how critical I was of certain of his characteristic ideas. But on the issue of the place of the historical Jesus in christology, I agreed with Tillich that faith and theology cannot rest on the life of the historical Jesus reconstructed by the use of the historical-critical method, but they do rest on the biblical picture of Jesus as the Christ portrayed by the evangelists and apostles. So when I met with Tillich, I asked him, "Now that I have passed my exams, what should I write on?" He answered, "It's clear to me. You should write on Martin Kähler, in particular his idea of 'the so-called historical Jesus and the historic biblical Christ,' " which happens to be verbatim the title of a little book Kähler published. The book attacks the whole sweep of modern critical scholarship that set out to discover the real Jesus of history in contrast to the kerygmatic Christ of the church.[6] Nothing in English had been written on Kähler and the Germans had not yet begun to assess the significance of his thought for subsequent theological developments. It was Kähler who first drew a distinction in theology between "Historie" and "Geschichte," and adopted the Greek word "kerygma" into the German language. In my dissertation on Martin Kähler I interpreted his thinking not only against the theological background of the nineteenth century but also in relation to his influence on Bultmann, Barth, and Tillich. I also concluded that Kähler's indictments against the "life of Jesus" movement of his own day would apply in large degree to the highly reductionistic portrayals of Jesus among the scholars of the New Quest. The historical Jesus of the post-Bultmannians does not look much like the "whole Christ of the whole Bible," to use Kähler's expression. Despite the theological motivation of the New Questers, their project was still very much a continuation of the Enlightenment project, only now framed by an existentialist hermeneutics.

The images of Jesus in the New Quest looked less Jewish than German and spoke "Heideggerian existentialese." In line with post-World War II West European consciousness, Jesus was portrayed as an utterly unique individual, thereby taking his historicity seriously. On this approach the task of scholarship is to focus on his will, his activity, his self-understanding, his intentionality, his way with others, and so forth. The terms ring with familiarity to anyone who has read the books and articles of the New Quest. Jesus' call for decision, exemplified in his own willingness to take a risk, climaxing in his death on the cross, became the core meaning of Easter. Jesus' continuation as a person after Easter was a function of the disciples' memories of their concrete experiences of Jesus before Easter. When Pannenberg raised the question, "Well, then, did Jesus really rise from the dead?" the New Questers professed not even to understand the question. They had fumbled the ball. Willi Marxsen was most bold among the post-Bultmannian New Questers to assert that the resurrection of Jesus means the continuation of his "cause" after his death. The resurrection becomes a predicate of the faith of Jesus' disciples, essentially a way of seeing, a perspectival view, rather than an event that happened to Jesus in the transition from the finality of death to a new form of eschatological life.

The New Quest is now a thing of the past. It failed both as an enterprise of critical, historical scholarship and as theological exegesis of the NT. Now it is as dead as Bultmannian existentialist hermeneutics with its individualistic *Fragestellung* [placing of the question] and neo-Protestant Vorverständnis [pre-understanding]. But lo and behold, now at the end of this century a "Third Quest" is underway. Its headquarters are no longer in Germany, but in the English speaking realm of theology. In this essay I intend to argue that all three quests have failed for the same fundamental reason. They have fallen into a chasm that separates Jesus from the church. Their approach to the historical Jesus suspends or brackets out the living reality of the church as the necessary condition of affirming the essential identity of the earthly Jesus and the risen Christ. The quest of the historical Jesus, new and old, proceeds on the assumption that Jesus is dead, a passive subject of historical investigation, best conducted by bracketing out the faith of his followers and their experience of his bodily presence in their eucharistic fellowship. The treatment of the resurrection, or lack of it, in the Jesus-research of today is a tell tale sign that the Enlightenment and not the faith of the church is in charge of the enterprise. Enlightenment presuppositions are decisive. "The Enlightenment," says Francis Schüssler Fiorenza, "rejected the claim of a special divine intervention or a supernatural revelation. It therefore denied the reality of miracles and especially the miracle of the resurrection of Jesus."[7] Apart from the resurrection as a real event in the experience of the person of Jesus, there can be no christology and thereby no way to bridge the gap between Jesus and his church. Christology and ecclesiology play no part in the Jesus books that claim to be written on the basis of strictly historical-scientific methods. While I believe that faith has a vital interest in the historical Jesus, I will reaffirm Kähler's point that the historical-critical method in the hands of faithless reason will produce only a "so-called historical Jesus," a product more of ideology than critical scholarship and of negative value to Christian faith and theology. Kähler did not reject the use of critical-historical methods in biblical studies, nor do I. Historical-critical inquiry into the gospel texts underscores the fact that Jesus of Nazareth was a real person of history, knowing full well that the method by itself cannot unveil the secret of his identity apart from belief in him as the Christ of God. Much hinges on whether the resurrection is fact or fable, history or myth. The rejection or neglect of the resurrection as historically real and true results in a separation between Jesus and Christ, between the fact of Jesus and his christological meaning. The legacy of Kantian epistemological dualism, the disjunction of fact and value, still underlies the scholars of the "Third Quest."

THE "THIRD QUEST" OF THE HISTORICAL JESUS

In spite of historical skepticism the search for the real Jesus of history goes on. N. T. Wright refers to the current movement beyond the New Quest as the "Third Quest."[8] We will adopt the term for the sake of convenience, but in our next section we will argue that from a theological point of view the Third Quest, like the Old and the New Quests, fails to take the resurrection of Jesus seriously as the necessary link to his own future as the risen Lord. Its concept of history is captive to historical positivism. What is sought is mere *"Historie"* and not *"Geschichte,"* dead history and not living history. Living history includes the horizon of the future. The real Jesus of history cannot be known in his fullness apart from the church and faith. Otherwise the Christ is separated from Jesus and lacks historical grounding and becomes an arbitrary postulate of faith in a Kantian sense. But we are getting ahead of ourselves.

The first striking resemblance between the Third Quest and the Old Quest is the sheer fantatistic variety of images of Jesus, all claiming to be based on documentary evidence and soberly sketched by using the most scientific methods of historical-critical scholarship. Of course, the plurality of images is nothing new. Jaroslav Pelikan in his book, *Jesus Through the Centuries,*[9] depicts the many faces of Jesus down through the centuries. In the setting of first-century Judaism, Jesus was seen as the eschatological Messiah; to the philosophical mind-set of Hellenism Jesus was the Logos, the rational principle of the universe. In Byzantine culture Jesus was the perfect icon of God; in medieval times Jesus was the monk modeling monastic discipline and self-denial; in mystical spirituality Jesus was the bridegroom of the soul; in the Reformation tradition Jesus is the Word of God whom the Spirit conveys in the living voice of the gospel *(viva vox evangelii)*; in liberal Protestantism Jesus is the perfect example of a socially enlightened morality. Schweitzer wrote an appropriate epitaph for how each age and each historian projected their own genius into their portrayals of Jesus: "Each successive epoch of theology found its own thoughts in Jesus; that was, indeed, the only way in which it could make him live. But it was not only each epoch that found its reflection in Jesus; each individual created him in accordance with his own character. There is no historical task which so reveals a man's true self as the writing of a life of Jesus."[10]

Schweitzer's words apply not only to the kaleidoscopic plurality of images in the history of Christianity and to the modern "Lives of Jesus" of the Old Quest, but also to our twentieth century interpretations of Jesus. "Which Jesus? Whose Jesus?" The modern quest of the historical Jesus began with a declaration of hostility to the church, its preaching about Jesus, its worship of him as the Son of God, and its dogma of the incarnation. Hans Conzelmann wrote in his article on Jesus Christ in the German theological encyclopedia, *Die Religion in Geschichte und Gegenwart*: "The historical and substantive presupposition for modern research into the life of Jesus is emancipation from traditional christological dogma on the basis of the principle of reason."[11] He was reiterating Schweitzer's judgment: "When at Chalcedon the West overcame the East, its doctrine of the two natures dissolved the unity of the Person, and thereby cut off the last possibility of a return to the historical Jesus.... This dogma had first to be shattered before men could once more go out in quest of the historical Jesus, before they could grasp the thought of his existence."[12] The religious and theological motive was to build a new Christianity, or perhaps even a new religion, on a historical Jesus freed from the church and its confession of Jesus as risen Lord.

The quest of the historical Jesus, old and new, aims to ascertain what can be discovered about Jesus in isolation from his community of believers, purely as the object of methodical, critical, historical research. The task is made difficult by the fact that Jesus appears to us exclusively through the medium of the church's memory and proclamation. The church's interest of faith was involved from the start in remembering, shaping, transmitting, gathering, and writing down all the words and events from Jesus' life, from both before and after his death on the cross. The resurrection of Jesus stands as the driving force behind the whole process giving rise to the NT. The recollections of the historical Jesus were preserved and passed on within the framework of the church's proclamation of Jesus as the risen Lord. All the gospels are witnesses of the early church. The "Third Quest" of the historical Jesus is very much like the Old Quest in that it aims to find the kernel of truth about Jesus, his very words, etc., inside the shell of the apostolic witness.

The process of separating out the authentic words of Jesus from the later constructions of the church inevitably calls for making scholarly judgments on the basis of certain presuppositions. There is no such thing as presuppositionless research. The answer to the questions, "Which Jesus? Whose Jesus?" cannot be given without coming clean on the matter of presuppositions. There were certain presuppositions at work in the formation of the gospel tradition in the life of the early church. Easter and Pentecost were the crucial ones. We know what we know about Jesus only in the light of Easter and Pentecost. If we invalidate them or neutralize them as functioning presuppositions in our approach to the historical Jesus, we will end up with a Jesus who looks very different from the Jesus Christ of the church's Book and the Christian tradition. Schweitzer was right: "The dogma had to be shattered before men could once more go out in quest of the historical Jesus." That is to say, everything that belongs to the church's faith and doctrine, life and history, must be removed—bracketed out—to carry on the quest of the historical Jesus. That seems to be the common methodological rule of those who search for the real Jesus of history in a purely historical-critical fashion.

The results of this "Third Quest" are not reassuring. For S. G. F. Brandon[13] Jesus was a political revolutionary, for Hugh Schonfield[14] a messianic schemer, for Morton Smith[15] the founder of a secret society, for C. F. Potter[16] a Qumran Essene, for Geza Vermes[17] a Galilean hasid, a holy man, for Burton Mack[18] a wandering Cynic preacher, for Dominic Crossan[19] a Mediterranean Jewish peasant, for Marcus Borg[20] a countercultural charismatic seeking the transformation of his social world, who fits right in with the new age spirituality of today, for Elizabeth Schüssler Fiorenza[21] Jesus was a feminist who called and formed his disciples into an egalitarian community of equals, for Barbara Thiering[22] a member of the Qumran community who married Mary Magdalene, had two sons and a daughter, divorced Mary and married another woman, and died some time in his 60's, for A. N. Wilson[23] a Galilean holy man who taught a simplified form of Judaism, minus its moralism and sectarianism, for Bishop John Spong[24] Jesus was born of a woman who had been raped, and all the stuff about Christmas and Easter in the gospels is nothing but the product of later Christian "midrash" and mythological speculation—what a promising foundation for an illustrious episcopal career! So again we ask: "Which Jesus? Whose Jesus?" Will the real Jesus please stand up?

More celebrated than any of these individual monographs is the group publication of scholars who formed the American "Jesus Seminar, " organized by Robert Funk of the Westar Institute. These scholars discussed the sayings of Jesus and voted with colored beads—red, pink, gray, and black—to determine their relative degree of certainty. Red meant certainly authentic: Jesus really said it; pink meant probably authentic: Jesus said something nearly like it; gray meant probably inauthentic: Jesus did not say it but it expresses his ideas; and black meant certainly inauthentic: Jesus did not say it and the saying is placed in the mouth of Jesus from a later time. Thus the historical Jesus arises out of the obscurity of the canonical gospels into the multi-colored light of scholarly reconstructions and probability judgments.

A THEOLOGICAL CRITIQUE OF THE "HISTORICAL JESUS" PROJECT

Jesus is, indeed, "the Man who belongs to the world."[25] As a world-historical figure the person of Jesus, together with his influence and reputation, cannot and will not be confined to Christianity. Those who are not believing Christians and members of Christ's church will see Jesus through their own spectacles, not respecting the kerygma, liturgy, and dogma of the church. Jews, Muslims, Buddhists, and Hindus will interpret the story of Jesus in light of their own beliefs about God and humanity, religion and morality. And so it is also to be expected that the academy of religious studies and biblical scholarship will do what it wants with Jesus, publishing their historical reconstructions of Jesus at whatever rate the market will bear. At the same time it is understandable that many believing Christians will respond to the plethora of exotic constructions and novelistic fantasies about the historical Jesus much like Mary Magdalene lamented to the two angels at the tomb, "They have taken away my Lord, and I do not know where they have laid him."[26]

On his way to a village in Caesarea Philippi, Jesus asked his disciples, "Who do people say that I am?" He followed that question with a second, "But who do you say that I am?" He did not expect the same answer to the two questions. He expected his disciples to know better than the people in general. When Peter shot back, "You are the Christ," Jesus told them to keep it a secret.[27] This exchange raises the question whether the historical-critical method, apart from any confessional submission to Jesus as the Christ within the communion of the church's experience, can best break open the secret of the true identity and meaning of Jesus for today .

Though the Bible is the "Book of the Church," and would not exist in its two-part canon of testaments without the church, it has become at the same time an open book that belongs to all humanity. It is a book of history—the history of Israel, the history of Jesus, and the history of primitive Christianity—that can be investigated by historians around the world, religious and non-religious, Christian and non-Christian scholars. They all bring their own perspectives to the question: "What can we know about Jesus?" But how can we really know which of the pictures of Jesus is objectively true—beyond subjectivism and relativism—that hang in the galleries of modern culture and religion? The historical-critical method is commonly regarded as the only adequate approach, using all the available sources and tools of modern critical scholarship. The sources and methods are public; they are not the private domain of the church. For Christian faith this is as it should be, following as a direct implication of taking seriously the full humanity of Jesus.

But does the historical-critical method suffice of itself? *The Christian Century* printed an exchange between John J. Collins, professor of Hebrew Bible at the University of Chicago, and Jon D. Levinson, a Jewish biblical scholar at Harvard Divinity School, on the competence of historical criticism in biblical interpretation.[28] John Collins reviewed Brevard S. Childs' *Biblical Theology of the Old and New Testaments*[29] and Jon D. Levinson's *The Hebrew Bible, The Old Testament and Historical Criticism: Jews and Christians in Biblical Studies.*[30] He criticized both of them for the same reason: they combine confessional faith with historical criticism. Collins writes: "Biblical scholars . . . regard a theological interest as at best irrelevant and at worst a distorting influence."[31] He goes on to say that the postulate of divine revelation on which faith and theology depend is irrelevant to historical criticism and can "only lead to obscurantism by cutting off the quest for a naturalistic, human explanation."[32] He adds, "A tendency toward historical distortion is inevitably present when one attempts to combine historical criticism with theological orthodoxy."[33] Collins finds Childs guilty of Barthian Protestantism and Levinson of orthodox Judaism. The alleged result is compromise. The confessional approach of Childs and Levinson, a Christian and a Jew, privileges certain theological commitments. "They are willing to participate fully in the historical-critical conversation so long as theological issues are not at stake."[34] Of Levinson's performance Collins writes: "His dalliance with historical criticism ends in *coitus interruptus,* since he pulls back before the final consummation."[35]

Jon Levinson answers Collins in a subsequent issue of the *Christian Century.*[36] Collins' position claims for historical criticism an exclusive and absolute access to the truth about the Bible, naively assuming that the principles underlying historical criticism are intrinsic to universal human reason and lie above and beyond the limits of historical relativity and cultural particularity.[37]

Levinson deals directly with the issue of historical criticism and the Bible in an article entitled, "The Bible: Unexamined Commitments of Criticism," which appeared in *First Things.*[38] The point he makes is that historical critics belong to a community of interpretation with its own prior assumptions—secular analogues to the religious commitments Jews and Christians bring to the text of the Bible. Those who think that the historical-critical method is value-neutral are self-deceived.

Ernst Troeltsch spelled out the fundamental principles of the historical-critical method: 1) the critical principle of methodological doubt; 2) the principle of analogy that says that all events are similar in principle; 3) the principle of correlation, the notion that all phenomena are inter-related and inter-dependent, subject to relations of cause and effect. Collins adds a fourth, the principle of autonomy, which means that neither church nor state can prescribe in advance what scholars must prove.

Collins thinks, says Levinson, that the commonly accepted "axioms of Troeltschian historicism are not 'prior commitments'."[39] Collins ignores the social character of knowledge. Historical critics operate with a set of assumptions that are no more self-evident and free of cultural particularism than the confessional commitments of Jews and Christians. Why should the church be asked to surrender its "prior commitments" anymore than the academy? Historical critics assume that they enjoy the privileged position of pursuing the truth wherever it may lead, without regard to any outside collectivity, religious or political. But in that they are fooling themselves. Levinson observes, "The academy has its own equivalents of excommunication and the revocation of membership."[40] Christian scholars should not be intimidated. Their commitments of faith have been condemned as irrelevant, obscurantist, or distortive by the positivistic historicists. It is time for them to challenge their secular colleagues to "fess up" to the prior assumptions of their own community of interpretation, and to admit that they lack grounds for making their supposedly value-neutral totalistic claims.[41]

The upshot of this exchange is that the historical-critical method does not exist as a naked and neutral set of research operations. It cannot through historical reconstruction build a bridge to our contemporary situation. A hermeneutical factor must come into play.

"Which hermeneutic? Whose hermeneutic?" That of the autonomous scholar who keeps his own confessional commitment private and hidden behind a cloak of positivistic historicism, or that of a community of faithful memory that forthrightly acknowledges the biblical writings as canonical? The fact of canon means that inquiry into the biblical texts—in this case, the quest of the historical Jesus—cannot be detached from the community that produced them and has kept them alive in an ongoing process of interpretation. In other words, if a hermeneutical factor is unavoidably entailed in every application of the historical-critical method, then it would seem reasonable to honor the tradition of interpretation of the religious community for which the Bible is more than a haphazard collection of ancient writings. Levinson warns biblical scholars of the folly of "sawing off the branch on which they are sitting."[42]

I am suggesting that the church is intrinsic to a hermeneutic of historical inquiry in search of the true identity and meaning of Jesus of Nazareth. This is clearly implied in Brevard Childs' "canonical method" of biblical interpretation, a method that Levinson endorses as equally applicable to the Jewish approach to the Hebrew Bible. The hermeneutical significance of the church in answering the question "Who was Jesus of Nazareth?" is also very evident in the writings of N. T. Wright, until recently a NT theologian at Worcester College, Oxford. In the preface of his little book, *Who Was Jesus?* Wright asserts: "Among other beliefs, I hold more firmly than ever to the conviction that serious study of Jesus and the gospels is best done within the context of a worshipping community."[43] An ecclesially oriented hermeneutic cannot produce facts that do not exist, nor can it use the historical-critical method merely to rubber stamp a belief system that existed prior to historical inquiry. But it does enter into the formation of scholarly judgments and decisions about matters of both fact and interpretation. I am not so sanguine as N.T. Wright about the theological promise of what he calls the "Third Quest," referring to the books about Jesus written by Geza Vermes, S. G. F. Brandon, E. P. Sanders, Marcus Borg, and others, but I do think that he is pushing Jesus-research in a theological direction that overcomes the "ugly ditch" that Lessing wrote about between historical facts and eternal truth, and which is reflected in the split between history and faith.

Although Wright prefers the "Third Quest" to the "Old" and the "New," he finds that it too is impaled on the separation of history and theology. Serious historical study of Jesus is the starting point for serious theological study, that is, the beginning of christology and the foundation of the church. And so he rightly faults the "Third Quest" for having nothing to say about Easter, and thereby failing to find the bridge connecting Jesus and the church. He says, "Serious historical research cannot remain silent here of all places."[44] Here the historical question is at the same time a matter of immediate theological concern. Wright says, "The central Christian claim is that Jesus of Nazareth was raised from the dead three days after his execution. I have argued . . . that as historians we are forced to take this claim very seriously indeed. The alternative explanations, when examined, turn out to be remarkably lame."[45] Why do the historical critics ignore or explain away what happened at Easter? Wright is correct in asserting: "There is a hole in the historical jigsaw-puzzle at just this point. One major test of any hypothesis about the history of the first century is how well it can cope with this hole."[46] Wright exposes the common opinion in almost all modern Jesus-studies—the assumption that because the resurrection is indeed a matter of faith, it cannot at the same time be a historical event. This assumption functions as a virtual dogma among historical critics and is subscribed to even by those who claim to be Christian. "The gospels (we are told) are faith-documents; therefore, they are not about history."[47] If something can be explained as belonging to the faith of the primitive Christian community, it must be subtracted from the Jesus-side of the ledger. But this will not work, because Jesus himself, his very being as the person he was, brings history and faith into the same focus. What we have in the NT is "theological history,"[48] and what the gospels narrate is not the story of the "historical

Jesus" who lurks like a ghost behind the texts to be reincarnated by modern critical historiography, but the canonical biblical Christ who is identical with the earthly Jesus.

ELEMENTS OF ECCLESIAL HERMENEUTICS

Theological historical exegesis is a function of the worshipping church. Outside the framework of the church, scholars will look for traces of a dead Jesus in first-century Palestine. Rabbi Peter Levinson of Heidelberg was quoted in *Time* magazine as saying: "If I believed in Jesus' resurrection, I would be baptized tomorrow."[49] Would that make a difference in what and how a scholar would write about Jesus? For example, Geza Vermes, a Jewish scholar, writes about Jesus in a way that can be fully accounted for within the limits of Judaism alone.[50] He concludes from his research that the church's confessions concerning Jesus Christ "have little to do with the religion preached and practiced by him."[51] It was the Christ of Paul and John who "overshadows and obscures the man of Galilee.... Jesus' eyes were fixed on God and his kingdom. Those of his followers, in particular Paul, focused on the risen and glorified Lord. The purely theocentric religion of Jesus became a christocentric faith in which the heavenly Father plays practically no role.... Is it an exaggeration to suggest that oceans separate Paul's Christian gospel from the religion of Jesus the Jew?"[52]

It is the appearance of Jesus of Nazareth as the risen Lord that distinguishes the perspective of Paul, a first century Jew, from that of Vermes, a twentieth century Jew. Paul and John, worse than Judas, are the ones who really betrayed Jesus. "John's Christ, " says Vermes, "had nothing in common with the real Jesus."[53] Vermes sees sheer discontinuity. John saw and expressed continuity between the earthly Jesus and the risen Christ in these words: "But the Advocate, the Holy Spirit, whom the Father will send in my name, will teach you everything, and remind you of all that I have said to you."[54] Appeal to the Spirit was also expressed by Paul: "So also no one comprehends what is truly God's except by the Spirit of God. Now we have received not the spirit of the world, but the Spirit that is from God, so that we may understand the gifts bestowed on us by God. And we speak of these things in words not taught by human wisdom but taught by the Spirit, interpreting spiritual things to those who are spiritual ."[55]

If Christian scholars bracket out the Holy Spirit alive and at work in the church, the community in which Christ is sacramentally present in his body and blood (the *totus Christus, caput et corpus*), their historical-critical treatments of the gospel narratives will probably become hermeneutically incoherent. Only the witness of the Spirit through the apostles can disclose the meaning of Jesus' life and death. Without the Spirit the historian at best would find only an empty grave on Easter, but no risen Savior. The outcome of a Spiritless hermeneutic of scripture is to interpret the life of Jesus in categories inappropriate to him. This phenomenon accounts in large part for the bewildering variety of modern images of Jesus—Jesus is a holy man, a revolutionary, a feminist, gay, black, a mushroom eater, a cross between a gnostic and a Cynic, etc., etc. Such interpretations of the historical Jesus are guided by extra-canonical paradigms dictated by the "elemental spirits of the age" (the *stoicheia*) and not the Holy Spirit of God and the Lord Jesus Christ.

Walter Kasper emphasizes the activity of the Spirit in overcoming the gulf between Jesus and the church. In an article, "The Church as Sacrament of the Spirit,"[56] Kasper corrects a one-sidedness found in the post-Bultmannian hermeneutics of Fuchs and Ebeling that places the quest of the historical Jesus exclusively within the framework of "Word and Faith" to the neglect of "Spirit and Church." The Eastern Orthodox emphasis on pneumatology in constructing both christology and ecclesiology offers a useful balance to the predominantly, if not exclusively, christological foundation of ecclesiology in both Protestant and Catholic forms of Western theology. It is only the experience of Jesus as the Christ in the power of the Spirit that founded and perpetuated the church after Jesus' death and resurrection.

But faith too is an essential link in the hermeneutical chain that connects Jesus and the church. *Fides quaerens intellectum!* Also with respect to the study of Jesus, faith is an element in the process of coming to knowledge. Philip Melanchthon coined the formula: "To know Christ is to know his benefits." Genuine Christian knowledge presupposes a living faith in the salvific presence of God incarnate in Jesus Christ. It is an immediate analytic judgment of faith that the person of Jesus is in some way homogeneous with the self-revealing God of Israel. The trinitarian and christological dogmas of the church express this truth in highly sophisticated ontological categories. An ecclesial hermeneutic will judge these dogmas as true interpretation of the historical Jesus who is at the same time the kerygmatic Christ. Church history illustrates that the abandonment of this orthodox ecclesial perspective leads either to judaizing christological tendencies on the left (ebionitism) or to gnosticizing tendencies on the right (docetism). Either Jesus was nothing but a mere man, or he was a supernatural ghost, not even human. The witness of the Holy Spirit (the *testimonium spiritus sancti internum)* creates the knowledge of faith concerning the true identity and meaning of Jesus Christ. In contrast, the historical Jesus reconstructed by critical scholarship never becomes more than a matter of higher or lower degrees of probability. Nothing is certain, so there can be no basis for the assurance of faith. A merely probable historical Jesus can never become the living Christ of faith. The Holy Spirit bridges faith and Christ by raising the historical Jesus out of the remoteness of past history into the context of contemporary ecclesial experience as the living Christ.

The living Christ becomes really present by the witness of the Holy Spirit in the experience of faith through the church's preaching of the Word. The evangelical reformation emphasis on "Word and Faith," however reductionistically it has developed in modern Protestantism, must be embraced in a more comprehensive catholic and orthodox hermeneutics of "Spirit and Church." The work of the Holy Spirit is not to "blow his own horn," but to serve as the inner dynamism of the living voice of the gospel of Christ *(viva vox evangelii)*. The Spirit is not a function of an individual's personal religious experience; he is rather the power of the preaching of Jesus as the Christ. Otherwise the words of preaching are only dead wires with no live current running through them!

Apart from the Spirit and the church there is no knowledge of the historical Jesus which has the power to awaken faith. Cyprian's formula is exactly right: *extra ecclesiam nulla salus*—outside the church there is no salvation! It seems somewhat odd that a Lutheran should be saying this when many Catholic scholars seemed to have abandoned it out of embarrassment. Apart from the church there is no communication concerning Jesus which can lead to a confession of him as Savior and Lord. The profane quest of the historical Jesus is not only powerless to awaken faith but may actually pose an obstacle in the way of grasping what is essential in the NT picture of Jesus of Nazareth .

The church is a sacrament and instrument of the Holy Spirit. The Holy Spirit not only works through the church, but the church is his dwelling place. Therefore, the church is the realm within which the true identity and meaning of Jesus can be known and confessed.

The "canonical method" of biblical interpretation to which we referred in the exchange between Jon Levinson and John Collins is usually associated with the name of Brevard Childs. Childs would not claim, however, that he invented the method. In its fundamental elements it has been the classical approach practiced within the liturgical and dogmatic life of the church. The "whole Christ of the whole Bible," and not some "historical Jesus" behind the scriptural texts, is the object of inquiry of the canonical method applied for the sake of the total life and worship of the church. The biblical texts in their final shape, just as they are, convey a trustworthy picture of Jesus as the One whom his apostles confessed as Lord and Savior. The simple Christian has access to this picture in the same way as a biblical scholar, even though he or she is unable to decompose the picture into the original elements which went into its making. It is the picture of the whole biblical Christ that has impressed itself on the memory of his community in the light of the Holy Spirit. The modern scholarly reconstructions of the historical Jesus are theologically suspect because they are used as substitutes for the apostolic picture of Jesus; they claim to set the record straight, to give us at last the historical truth about the real Jesus of Nazareth, which is a different Jesus than the person we meet in the apostolic preaching of Jesus as the Christ.

CONCLUSION

We have come to the end of our reflection on the relevance of ecclesial hermeneutics for the quest of the historical Jesus. Our theological critique of the quest in all its manifestations was offered in light of an approach which we have variously referred to as "ecclesial hermeneutics," "theological exegesis," or the "canonical method." But this approach finally hinges on the issue of the authority of the Bible as the Word of God. And that is to introduce another topic. We will conclude, however, by putting it forward as an inescapable issue. The authority of scripture lies at the heart of our concept of ecclesial hermeneutics. The uniqueness and authority of scripture are meaningless concepts to biblical critics for whom early Christianity is just one of several Hellenistic propaganda religions or for whom the biblical writings can be interpreted exhaustively within the arena of human experience and human reason .

Last fall the Pontifical Biblical Commission issued a document entitled, *The Interpretation of the Bible in the Church.*[57] This document provides a strong affirmation of the historical-critical method of exegesis; yet, it warns exegetes of the dangers of ignoring the believing community as the truly adequate context for interpreting the canonical scriptures. In this context faith, the Holy Spirit, and church authority are necessary to remain faithful to the great tradition that produced the canon. The canonical writings, says the document, possess "a salvific and theological value completely different from that attaching to other ancient texts."[58] It recognizes "the fact that the Holy Spirit is the principal author of the Bible," and that the light of the Spirit and faith lived in ecclesial community are needed to be faithful to the revelation of God attested by the Bible. These are the perennial presuppositions of a hermeneutics that deliberately places itself within the living tradition of the church. If biblical scholars do not proceed with such an ecclesial preunderstanding in their historical and exegetical work, they have the burden of proving that any alternative set of presuppositions is better suited for the task of biblical interpretation. The church has a long record of experience in reading, rereading and recontextualizing the scriptures and will not be easily convinced that it has missed the mark from the moment it began to translate its memories into manuscript and on through the subsequent centuries of biblical interpretation.

NOTES

1. Albert Schweitzer, *The Quest of the Historical Jesus*, trans. by W. Montgomery, 3rd ed. (London: Adam & Charles Black, 1954).

2. Paul Tillich, *Systematic Theology* (Chicago: The University of Chicago Press, 1957), II, 102.

3. Rudolf Bultmann, *Jesus and the Word*, trans. by Louise Smith and Erminie Lantero (New York: Charles Scribner's Sons, 1934), 9.

4. Emil Brunner, *The Mediator*, trans. by Olive Wyon (Philadelphia: The Westminster Press, 1947), 187.

5. Ernst Käsemann, "The Problem of the Historical Jesus," in *Essays on New Testament Themes*, Studies in Biblical Theology, no. 41, trans. by W. J. Montague (Naperville, Ill.: Alec R. Allenson, 1964), 46.

6. Martin Kähler, *Der sogenannte historische Jesus und der geschichtliche, biblische Christus* (Leipzig: A. Deichert, 1896.) The book was reissued in 1956 by Christian Kaiser Verlag, Munich. The English translation appeared in 1964 by Fortress Press, translated, edited, and with an introduction by Carl E. Braaten. I tried to capture the flavor of Kähler's distinction between "historisch" and "geschichtlich" by the English words "historical" and "historic," respectively.

7. Francis Schüssler Fiorenza, *Foundational Theology. Jesus and the Church* (New York: Crossroad, 1984), 5.

8. N. T. Wright, *Who Was Jesus?* (Grand Rapids: Wm B. Eerdmans Publishing Company, 1993), 12.

9. Jaroslav Pelikan, *Jesus Through the Centuries* (New Haven: Yale University Press, 1985).

10. Schweitzer, 4.

11. *RGG*, 3rd ed. (1959) ET, *Jesus* (Philadelphia: Fortress Press, 1973), 5.

12. Schweitzer, 3.

13. S. G. F. Brandon, *Jesus and the Zealots: A Study of the Political Factor in Primitive Christianity* (Manchester: The University Press, 1967).

14. Hugh J. Schonfield, *The Passover Plot* (London: Hutchison & Co., 1965).

15. Morton Smith, *The Secret Gospel: The Discovery and Interpretation of the Secret Gospel According to Mark* (New York: Harper, 1973).

16. C. F. Potter, *The Last Years of Jesus* (New York: Fawcett Publications, 1958).

17. Geza Vermes, *Jesus the Jew: A Historian's Reading of the Gospels* (New York: The Macmillan Company, 1973).

18. Burton H. Mack, *A Myth of Innocence: Mark and Christian Origins* (Philadelphia: Fortress Press, 1988).

19. John Dominic Crossan, *The Historical Jesus: The Life of a Mediterranean Jewish Peasant* (San Francisco: Harper & Row, 1991).

20. Marcus Borg, *Jesus: A New Vision* (San Francisco: Harper & Row, 1987).

21. Elizabeth Schüssler Fiorenza, *In Memory of Her; A Feminist Theological Reconstruction of Christian Origins* (New York: Crossroad, 1983).

22. Barbara Thiering, *Jesus the Man: A New Interpretation from the Dead Sea Scrolls* (Sydney, Australia: Doubleday, 1992).

23. A. N. Wilson, *Jesus* (London: Sinclair-Stevenson, 1992).

24. John Spong, *Born of a Woman: A Bishop Rethinks the Birth of Jesus* (San Francisco: Harper & Row, 1992).

25. Pelikan, 220.

26. John 20:13b.

27. Mark 8:27-30.

28. "Historical Criticism and the State of Biblical Theology," *Christian Century*, July 28-August 4, 1993, 743-747.

29. Brevard S. Childs, *Biblical Theology of the Old and New Testaments: Theological Reflection on the Christian Bible* (Minneapolis: Fortress Press, 1993).

30. Jon D. Levinson, *The Hebrew Bible, The Old Testament and Historical Criticism: Jews and Christians in Biblical Studies* (Philadelphia: Westminster/John Knox Press, 1993).

31. Collins, 743.

32. Ibid., 744.

33. Ibid., 746.

34. Ibid., 747.

35. Ibid.

36. "Biblical Criticism: An Exchange," *Christian Century*, 30, October 13, 1993, 994-997.

37. Ibid., 995.

38. Jon D. Levinson, "The Bible: Unexamined Commitments of Criticism, *First Things*, (February, 1993), 24-33. This article appeared in a somewhat different version in his book, *The Hebrew Bible, the Old Testament, and Historical Criticism: Jews and Christians in Biblical Studies*..

39. *First Things*, 30.

40. Ibid., 31.

41. Ibid., 32.

42. Ibid., 32.

43. Wright, ix.

44. Ibid., 18.

45. Ibid., 81.

46. Ibid., 59.

47. Ibid., 95.

48. Ibid., 96.

49. "Resurrection: A Jew Looks at Jesus, *Time*, May 7, 1979, 95.

50. Cf. Geza Vermes, *Jesus the Jew* (London: Collins, 1973) and, twenty years later, *The Religion of Jesus the Jew* (Minneapolis: Fortress, 1973).

51. *The Religion of Jesus the Jew*, 210.

52. Ibid., 210, 211, 212.

53. Ibid., 213.

54. John 14:26.

55. 1 Cor 2:11b-13.

56. Cf. Walter Kasper and Gerhard Sauter, *Kirche—Ort des Geistes* (Freiburg: Herder, 1976), 12-55.

57. The English text is available in *Origins*, CNS Documentary Service, January 6, 1994, Vol. 23: No. 29, 497-524.

58. Ibid., 515.

THE VOICE OF GOD'S PEOPLE IN EXILE

STANLEY D. WALTERS

This paper is an interpretive exposition of Hannah's prayer in 1 Sam 2:1-10. I have deemed it suitable for a symposium on the general theme of the church because I believe the book of Samuel—for the two books of Samuel form a literary whole—is about the life and institutions of the church in a time beyond kingship, namely, worship, preaching, and hope for the King to come.

EXILE

To read the Bible as scripture is to read it as speaking to us in our own concrete situation. The terms "exile" and "dispersion" come increasingly to the mind of Christians as we observe the decline of the church as an institution of prominence and privilege in our society. My perspective is that of an American, resident in Canada since 1976, and particularly in the multicultural and pluralistic Toronto (which, someone says, will in fifteen years be a nonwhite city). Everywhere special interests contend for their own rights and standing; the Christian church, as the entrenched institution, must often yield its status, sometimes rightly, sometimes unfairly, but usually to the effect of weakened identity, diminished visibility, and blunted witness.

I also reflect the troubled state of the churches. A denominational official who has recently ended an endowment drive, not very successful, and who has been inside many congregations during the past three years, says that the domimant characteristics he has seen there are conflict and fear. *Conflict,* amongst the people or between the people and the clergy, and *fear,* of decline, of change, of failure, of the future.

"Exile" is, of course, a metaphor, based on Israel's experience in the sixth century B.C. That was a time of dislocation and disorder more severe than we in North America have experienced: God's people, having lived and died for centuries in their own land under at least nominal allegiance to the covenant, having run the government and set the tone of national life, now began life as displaced peoples in someone else's society. As Christians in North America begin to feel the running of government and the tone of national life moving farther and farther from their grasp and control, the metaphor of exile seems more and more appropriate.

I. HANNAH'S PRAYER

I offer, first, a translation of the masoretic text of this prayer and an analytic outline and then will move to the exposition.

A. Translation of 1 Sam 2:1-10

1. Then Hannah prayed this prayer:

My heart exults in the LORD,
Through the LORD my head is high,
My mouth rebukes my enemies,
Because I rejoice in y deliverance.

2. There is none holy like the LORD,
Indeed, there is no one but you,
No, there is no rock like our God.

3. Enough of your talking
So big, so big! Enough arrogance from your mouth!
For the LORD is a God well-informed,
He has sized up your behavior.

4. The bows of heroes are broken,
The faltering have belted on strength.
5. Those filled with food must get a job,
And the starving hunger no more.
Even the barren has borne seven,
But the mother of many is in despair.

6. The LORD kills and makes alive,
He brings down to Sheol, he brings up.
7. The LORD impoverishes and makes rich,
He brings low, yes, he exalts.
8. He raises the poor from the dust,
From the trash heaps he lifts the needy,
To seat them with nobles;
Yes, he grants them a glorious seat.

For earth's very pillars are the LORD'S,
He placed the world upon them.
9. He guards the feet of his faithful,
While the wicked are silenced in darkness,
For one cannot prevail by human strength.

10. The LORD! His adversaries will be shattered,
Against him he thunders in the heavens.
The LORD judges the ends of the earth,
Giving strength to his king
And lifting the head of his anointed.

B. Introduction

1. The starting point for my interpretation is that Hannah is God's people. This is

based, first, on the Bible's frequent use of a woman to represent Israel, starting with the matriarchs whose barrenness God overcame in order that there should be Israelites at all—the people of God are the gift of God—and continuing with such passages as Isa 54:1 where Jerusalem is specifically a barren woman, and Jer 31:15 where Rachel is the northern kingdom, mourning the loss of her children. It is also an inference from 1 Sam 1 and its midrashic use of the verb *šāʾal* "ask," which establishes a cross-reference to Deut 18:16 where, at Horeb, God's people "ask" for a mediator between themselves and the speaking God and receive the promise of a prophet like Moses. It is now Hannah who also "asks," and the promise of Deut 18:16 is the mysterious "word" which her husband Elkanah expects God to fulfill (1 Sam 1:23) and which Samuel's birth does fulfill. That is to say, by these allusions, the narrative itself construes her as God's people.

A prayer for God's people to offer is a prayer for us, for that is who we are when we read the Bible as scripture. We are the people the text addresses and to whom it offers itself for guidance and tutelage.

The book Samuel may well be considered as "history," but we do not now read it first of all to reconstruct the events between the judges and the kingship. It may well give us a window on interesting social customs and cultic practices, but we do not now read it as anthropologists in order to describe ancient Israel's institutions. We are not antiquarians; we are God's people in dispersion, desperate to know how to live before God and within our own society. We are this Hannah.

2. This brings us to the position of the poem within the larger narrative. It is a fruitful question to ask of any text—and often difficult to answer—Why is it where it is? Hannah offers her prayer *after* presenting Samuel to Eli for God's service at the sanctuary (1:26-27), and *before* leaving for home (2:11). The prayer does not follow Eli's promise that she would receive her request; there, "her face showed the difference," and she took food (1:18-19). It does not follow Samuel's birth, where her only response was to connect his birth with her prayer (1:20). She prays only after she had finally weaned him, presented him to Eli, and was ready to return home without him.

Her praise, therefore, is not just for the personal answer to prayer and the reversal of her standing in the home. It is for *all she believes Samuel will be*: a person given and desired by God (1:27-28), and a faithful priest (2:35) who will be the means of renewing God's people through godly leadership at the sanctuary. The prayer's position envelops it with cultic activity and concerns. Before, chapter 1 is a thoroughly cultic story of pilgrim worship, priestly oracle, and dedication of Samuel to the priesthood. After the prayer the rest of chapter 2 shows him serving God and contrasts him repeatedly and directly with the cavalier and profligate Hophni and Phinehas. Insofar as the prayer has to do with Hannah's specific situation, she praises God for the priestly Samuel.

But God's gift was larger than Hannah envisioned, something we do not ourselves know without reading the story and reflecting on its cross-references and allusions. Hannah's praise, therefore, is also for *all that the narrative knows Samuel will be*: a faithful prophet (3:20) calling God's people to penitence, obedience, and integrity (3:19-21; 7; 12), the maker of Israel's first two kings and—in the book that bears his name—the teacher of Israel's theology and the framer of messianic hope.

Although we rightly know Samuel as the archetypal prophet, he combines in himself—in Hannah's expectation and in his own practice as well—the two offices of priest and prophet. The framing of the prayer with cultic-prophetic stories thus matches the book's larger picture of Samuel, as well as the book's framing with cultic-prophetic stories (1 Sam 1.1, and 2 Sam 2.24). It follows that the prayer celebrates much more than the answer to a single prayer. It celebrates the epochal importance to God's people of the gifts of worship and preaching.

3. Finally, we note that Hannah prayed (2:1). Commentators usually refer to this text as her "song." It is, of course, like the biblical psalms in its poetic character; a few lines even reappear in Psalm 113, and biblical psalms can also be called "prayers" (Ps 72:20). At the end of Samuel, in a poem virtually identical with Psalm 18, David will speak the words of a "song" (*šîrâ,* 2 Sam 22:1 = Ps 18). But Hannah "prayed."

The verb *hitpallel* "pray" has been important in the story of Samuel's birth, where it occurs five times alongside the key verb "ask." It denoted there Hannah's desperate request for a son, a petition God has now answered in Samuel, one who is more than she yet knows. The verb now occurs again. Hannah's words are a prayer in that they bear human thoughts to God, but here they are visionary rather than petitionary. There is not a single verb in this prayer that petitions, it is not a request but a declaration. This is probably one of the reasons that the Old Greek reads simply, "She said."

Among other things, this affects our understanding of praying. "Prayer" is the genus, "ask" is the species. It also serves, however, to draw Hannah into the prophetic orbit in which prayer has a distinct role. Her words are prophetic, not in any sharply predictive sense but in their confidence that God's rule intends human equity, will not be ultimately frustrated, and will be finally implemented in God's coming order through his designated Anointed One.

Thus Hannah becomes a prophetess. The targum carries the role to elaborate lengths. It says, "She prayed, *in a spirit of prophecy,*" and adds *predictions* to the *declaration* of the biblical text. She shows advance knowledge of the Assyrian king Sennacherib, of the Babylonian Nebuchadnezzar, of Mordecai and Esther (i.e. the Persian period), of the Greeks and the Hasmoneans, of the Romans, and even of the eschatological enemy Gog. Since the LXX calls Hannah by the Greek name *Avva* (with rough breathing), we will not be surprised to find in a later temple a woman by that name, called a "prophetess," speaking about the eight-day-old Jesus "to all who were hoping for the redemption of Jerusalem" (Luke 2:36-38).

By contrast, the Old Greek is an earthly poem. It has an insertion dealing with human boasting and closes by stating that God will give strength, not to "his king," as in the MT, but to "our kings."

4. Opening and Closing. The prayer is bracketed by two references to a "high horn" (translated idiomatically as "head is high" in v. 1), a figure drawn from the animal world and implying vigor and confidence. The text reads literally: "my horn is high in the LORD" (v. 1b), and, "[the LORD] will make high the horn of his anointed" (v. 10e). The prayer opens with Hannah and closes with the King. It opens with her own personal praise and closes with a confident assertion of God's victory over every adversary and of his sovereign rule. It opens in Shiloh; it closes at the ends of the earth. It opens with a local reversal; it closes with a cosmic reversal. It opens in the present age; it closes with the age to come.

The prayer is therefore like the book Samuel itself, especially as the opening and closing poems guide our understanding. Hannah's prayer and David's song (2 Sam 22) are poetic compositions standing in the second and next to last positions of the book. At the beginning of the book, God's people pray. At its close, the Anointed One sings.

5. Summary. When Hannah offers this prayer, then, we know what God's people should say as they live the life of the covenant under the gifts of torah and prophecy in a world beyond earthly king and kingship. They will *pray,* guided by the offices of priest and prophet. If we may be analytic about the movement of ideas in her prayer, this implies something like the following.

a. We praise God: through descriptive praise, for the gifts of priest and prophet, and through confessional praise, for the very divine being.

b. We rebuke the arrogant speech of those within the covenant who are unsubmissive to torah and prophecy and whose deeds do not pass God's muster.

c. We affirm—again, both descriptively and confessionally—the equitable order which God seeks and will have and towards which obedience to torah and prophecy carries us.

d. We look in hope towards God's intervention to do what even covenant obedience cannot fully accomplish and to bring the King to come who will rule and prosper in divine strength.

In bringing to Hannah's voice the larger sphere of God's rule in the world, both now and in the future, the prayer tells us that the whole story of Samuel, Saul, and David has to do not just with her, but with God's long plan for the covenant people, for our life in the world, and for the world itself. *This is the subject matter of the book:* the life of God's people under worship, prophecy, and coming kingship. God's desired order will come through obedience to torah and prophecy and, ultimately, through the King who comes. Samuel is about our suffering, our struggles, our hopes.

C. Outline

I suggest the following outline for the prayer:

- A. Praise to God
    - 1. Descriptive praise for God's deliverance (v. 1)
    - 2. Confessional praise for God's character (v. 2)
- B. Protest to "You" (plural) (v. 3)
    - 1. Arrogant speech must end
- C. Reversal of human circumstances (vs. 4-5)
    - 1. Descriptive: representative reversals (vs. 4-5)
      The verbs have human subjects and there are three pairs of specific contrasts.
    - 2. Confessional: God's action effects reversal (vs. 6-8d)
      The verbs have "the LORD" as subject.
        - a. Four pairs of general contrasts (vs .6-7)
        - b. God honors the poor and needy (vs. 8a-d)
- D. God's continuing triumph through his King (vs. 8e-10)
    - 1. God has founded the world (vs. 8e-f)
    - 2. God deals with the faithful and the wicked (vs. 9a-c)
    - 3. God prevails through his King (v. 10)

II. EXPOSITION

What do we do and say as we live our lives before God and within our own world?

A. Praise to God

First, the voice of God's people gives praise. Following the biblical patterns, we offer praise to God in two forms: *joyous* description of God's actions for us, and *joyous acknowledgement* of God's character and attributes. We may call them simply *testimony* and *adoration*, and they are among the proper elements of all prayer.

1. *Testimony* (v. 1)

In the first three lines of the prayer Hannah first speaks of her attitude to God, then towards herself and her own confidence, and finally towards her "enemies." The first three sections of the psalm—A.1, A.2, B.—correspond to this general reference. Verse 1 offers the prayer's only lines in which Hannah makes a direct appearance as a person; once she moves on to the character of God (v. 2), the "I/my" words disappear; in v. 3, using plural verbs, she turns outward to certain other people. These are the three primary relationships of life: God, self, others, although in reality they are circles that always intersect and overlap.

In v.1, the verbs of all four lines describe Hannah's own state; these are new conditions, in contrast to those of chapter 1. In that part of the story, she prayed in bitterness of soul and with weeping (1:10) and in "great anguish and distress" (1:18); now she exults. There, she suffered Peninnah's taunts, wept and could not face food (1:7), and described herself as a desperate woman (1:15); now she feels confident and strong. There, although Peninnah sought "to provoke an outburst" (1:6), we hear no words but those of Hannah's prayer (1:11); now her "mouth is wide."

By its idiom, each line keeps her at one remove from these new conditions: it is her *heart* that exults, her *horn* that is high, her *mouth* that is wide. But then, she herself becomes the direct subject of a verb so that v. 1e comes almost as a shout: "I rejoice! "

We hear of "enemies," even as we do in many biblical psalms. Their identity is always elusive. In chapter 1 the only possible human enemy is Peninnah, but the prayer uses the plural. Hophni and Phinehas and the religious disorders at Shiloh are included as well. Although the story does not describe them until 2:12-17, 22-26, they are already implicit through the names of the three priests in 1:3. Nor is Hannah speaking of people alone, but of all she has been through: the other woman, certainly, but also her barrenness, the reproach, the shortfall in understanding from Elkanah and from Eli, her bitterness and desperation, and, after Samuel's birth, the struggle to keep her promise. These are the enemies whose assault she has withstood and towards whom she opens wide her mouth.

Even though the prayer speaks here of our own feelings, these lines never lose sight of God. Two important details show this. First, the name of Israel's God, YHWH, "the LORD," stands in both lines 1b and 1c. The NRSV, following the Greek, changes the second to "my God," doubtless in order to obtain a pleasing variation (as in 2 Sam 22:7). But the Hebrew text is rhetorically slightly more austere, and, since the divine name YHWH cannot carry the possessive suffix "my," the effect is both to keep attention on God as the sovereign actor and slightly to relativize the human persona in the giving of praise.

Second, addressing God directly, we rejoice "in your deliverance" (line 1e), that is, the deliverance accomplished by God. The NRSV reads "my victory"; both the pronoun and the chosen equivalent change the meaning sharply. The reading "my" follows a single manuscript from Qumran, against the MT and the LXX, and I do not consider it defensible. To say *"your* deliverance" keeps attention on the divine action rather than on the human situation, now changed; testimony to God's blessing properly focuses on God the Giver rather than on the receiver. It also widens the reference of "deliverance." To say "your *deliverance*" makes it possible to think of all that God does through the gift of prophecy implicit in Samuel's birth, while to say "my *victory*" (NRSV) is to refer only to the birth of Samuel and its effects within Hannah's home. By further extension into the book's hope for the future, "deliverance" also intimates the King to come with which the prayer closes (v. 10). God's sovereign rule in the world expresses itself in individual victories won for God's people, which are also foretastes of the more perfect realization of that rule which is still to come.

2. *Adoration* (v. 2)

From the very personal language of v 1, the song moves exclusively to God, confessing the divine incomparability by means of two complementary lines using the words, "holy" and "rock."

a. No single word better comprises what it means that God is God than *qādôš* "holy." It implies an absolute otherness arising from absolute moral purity and excellence. Israel's God, YHWH, "the LORD," possesses this quality as does no other being in heaven or on earth, so much so that "there is no God but you." We know already (v. 1) that the LORD is a God at hand, who saves and who fills us with exultation and rejoicing. Now we celebrate that divine being as "holy," unique in flaming purity, dwelling "in light inaccessible, hid from our eyes."

It is this *holiness* that gives rise to God's saving actions, rather than divine *justice*. The Greek version introduces the idea of justice at several points: here in v. 2 (where, instead of "... there is no *rock* like our God," it reads, "...there is no *just one* like our God") and three other times, in additions to the poem in vs. 8 and 10. It is part of the more earthly character of the Greek version, which also adds several lines on proper and improper boasters and associates the idea of justice with the need to discriminate between them.

Justice is a concept associated in our own time very strongly with human well-being, especially in the expression "social justice," and the ethics of the biblical covenant require equitable and fair treatment of all people. But human justice is not an absolute value; God is not guided or bound by it, but by his own character of holy love. God's holiness is the source of his own justness and is the only ultimate guarantee of human justice. If we regard God's justice as primary, we may feel that we have a right to be treated fairly; if we make God's *holiness* primary, we know that God expects us to live a moral life. In that the Hebrew version of the prayer does not refer to justice, it lodges salvation deeper in the divine character (so to speak), so that it is God's holiness which effects the reversals of human station in vs. 4-8. This leads me to suppose—as we will see—that the reversals of vs. 4-8d are not arbitrary or whimsical, but in keeping with God's own character.

b. The third line of v. 2 brings God close, after emphasizing in the first line his otherness and purity. With the wording *"our* God," the possessive pronoun *both* bridges the distance implicit in "holy" *and* shifts attention away from me, the individual who exults, onto the group gathered in loyalty around the covenant.

God is also the "rock." In addition to a quality—"holy"—full of meaning but abstract, God is a concrete noun. In addition to an adjective, clear enough but predicative, God is a bold metaphor.

The word *ṣûr* "rock" occurs in the Bible sixty-six times, overwhelmingly associated with God. In about half of these passages, it is a direct substitute for or epithet of God. For example: "The Rock!—His deeds are perfect" (Deut 32:4), and "Exalted be God, the Rock/Who gives me victory" (2 Sam 22:47). The language with which the word occurs in these passages shows that God as Rock implies *strength and shelter*.. Most of the remaining passages are *providential* or *revelatory*. An example of the providential *ṣûr* would be the rock from which God brought water to quench thirst in the desert; an example of the revelatory *ṣûr* would be the rock from which Moses beheld God's glory. Even in these cases, the word *ṣûr* probably carries the double meaning "Rock/God." In only a few passages does it seem to denote mountainous terrain and no more.

As an image, then, the rock of this confessional praise identifies God with the massiveness of the mountains so as to imply great safety and security, but also draws in, through the miracles of providence and divine self-disclosure, God's care and nourishment of the people of the covenant and even the remarkable willingness of God to disclose to them something of his own character.

A God who combines the passionate purity of "holy" with the compassionate safety and sustenance of "rock," is indeed incomparable, and the middle line of this verse makes of this peerless deity a "thou" of direct adoration. The statement is categorical and almost credal: "There is no God but you." It does not envisage a world of gods from which a choice might be made. Israel's God is alone in what he does and is, and by that divine character and action God's people are led to acknowledge him as the sole being with the right to be called "God" and to act in the world to accomplish the divine design.

B. Protest (v 3)

The voice of God's people protests arrogant speaking. The prayer now turns from praise to protest, and we hear what it means for our mouth to be "wide" against our enemies. These words would be appropriate if addressed to the rival wife Peninnah, who habitually sought—without success—to provoke Hannah to an outburst (Hebrew "to make her thunder," 1:6). The verbs and pronouns, however, are plural; if Peninnah is included, so are others. In the narrative of chapter 1, Hannah never replied to Peninnah, and the rival is not present in Shiloh as she prays. Hannah here addresses the wider world of arrogant speakers. The domestic provocation she suffered is the tip of an iceberg: it is but part of a large, frigid, destructive mass of hostile speaking.

Verbal abuse is a frequent feature of human distress, whether spoken by the people closest to us (Ps 55:13-15, 21-22; 41:6-10) or by others (Ps 22:7-9; 64:3-6), and God's people as a group also experience it (Ps 44:14; 74:10,18; 79:4). Derisive talk is the chief and most effective form of social pressure.

I read the protest here in the light of the importance of speech in the Bible. Before the world was, there was speaking; before the cosmos existed, there was utterance. The second line in the Bible tells us, "God said." In the beginning was the Speaker.

Not only that, but the first recounted action of the world's first person involved speaking: the human gave names to the animals. His second action was the same. When God brought to him the newly-created woman, what was the response? Not a hug, not a kiss, not a roll in the grass. No, *"The man said"* (Gen 2:23). Maybe we would have written the story differently, but there it is. The first humans were created speaking, doubting, even lying. In the beginning was the speaker.

In the biblical story, then, which we take as a guide to our best understanding of how things are and ought to be, to speak is the first thing that God did and the first thing done by human beings. To speak is to perform a godlike act. It is a primary characteristic of God and in people a mark of creation in God's image. To learn is human, to speak is divine. The point of God's speaking was to replace chaos with order. God spoke, and we hear the results in the marvelously ordered and patterned creation story with which the Bible opens. It follows that with us as with God, the proper effect of speaking is to order the life we know and must live.

Hannah's prayer of adoration (vs. 1-2) and social vision (vs. 4-8d) exemplifies the fundamental purpose of the divine gift of speaking: to praise the living God our Creator and to establish with other human beings a community of shared meanings—a community accountable to the God who is holy and guaranteed by God the Rock. Thus speaking seeks its created purpose: order under God.

The text puts it negatively because to speak arrogantly is to use speaking *against* these two created purposes, releasing into the world centers of intention and invention—that is, words—that do not acknowledge the Creator's claims upon us and that create disorder rather than order. When that happens, we have set foot on the vertiginous slope of hubris: "I will speak as I please ... I am God."

Whoever speaks abusively to God's people does so to God as well. Arrogant and duplicitous speech is one of the principal marks of God's enemies, and especially of the arrogant oppressor whose role is that of the anti-messiah. Doeg the Edomite is the prototype, and the character is developed in the visions of Daniel and John. Actual oppressors certainly informed these latter descriptions, but they remain nameless in the Bible, showing that they are figures for all that is hostile towards God and especially for those monstrous embodiments of evil who qualify as "antichrists."

From exuberant praise, the scene has shifted to a world where both people and God encounter aggressive, arrogant speech. It seems to me that these speakers are first of all people within the covenant. Peninnah lived in the same house. Just as Hannah is a figure for God's faithful, so Peninnah is a figure for those from whom they suffer hostile and derisive verbal attack. The most telling opposition to the renewal of God's people is the hostile, often whispered, criticisms from within. The protest of v. 3, then applies to all those whose hostile talk threatens God's people and obstructs God's plan. Its force is not psychological but theological; the larger text is a prayer. Our poise and confidence in the face of hostile talk is that God is well-informed, can easily size up the situation, and will in his own time set things right.

C. Reversal of Human Circumstances (vs. 4-8d)

The voice of God's people envisions God's equitable order. The central segments of the prayer speak of certain striking reversals in people's lives.

This material comes before us in two ways. First, descriptively, there are three pairs of explicit contrasts in which people experience dramatic reversal in life's circumstances (six poetic lines, vs 4-5). People are themselves the subject of these verbs, but the means by which the changes occur is not expressed; for example, "The barren has borne seven," and "the mother of many is in despair." Second, confessionally, there are four pairs of briefer contrasts stating the LORD'S power to make such changes (four poetic lines, vs. 6-7). "The LORD" is the subject of the verbs; for example, "The LORD kills and makes alive." Four further lines describe God's lifting of the poor and needy to a state of honor (v. 8a-d).

1. *Representative reversals* (vs. 4-5)

Vs. 4-5 are *descriptive*, giving three pairs of contrasting human conditions each of which is reversed. We hear that people with great strength and prowess, plentiful food, and large families suffer shocking deprivation. Similarly, the conditions of physical weakness, hunger, and lack of children are reversed. One is a reversal of macho male prowess—"The bows of heroes are broken, the faltering have belted on strength." One is a reversal of female longing—"Even the barren has borne seven, but the mother of many is in despair." And one is gender-neutral and universal: "Those filled with food must get a job, and the starving hunger no more."

The sequence of six reversals follows the order negative/positive, negative/positive, positive/negative, giving a slight tilt towards negative reversal through the opening and closing lines of vs. 4-5.

Instances of some of these reversals take place right within Samuel, For example, Goliath's fall (1 Sam 17); the defeat of Absalom's revolt (2 Sam 15-18); and David's recovery from the humiliation of that revolt and from his unseemly grief (2 Sam 19:2-9). Loss of livelihood is predicted for Eli's descendants (1 Sam 2:36), and a famine at the end of the book comes to conclusion (2 Sam 21:1-14). Finally, the barren Hannah bears children (1 Sam 2:21), while two mothers suffer the combined loss of their seven sons (2 Sam 21:8).

But the function of these contrasts is not to forecast the events of the book; if it were, it fails, for Hannah bears six children, not seven, and there is no intimation that Peninnah suffered despair. This immediate and obvious disparity shows that the prayer's reference lies beyond the narrative sequence of Samuel.

Nor are these lines a general program of social levelling and reform. Their sweeping and absolute character is very striking. There are no qualifications or conditions mentioned. The elevated states which are reversed are not evil or negative in themselves. What kind of equality does God want in our world? A world in which there are no heroes, but no stumblers either (v. 4)? A world of bland and blessed uniformity, with everyone equally mediocre and mild? A world of no mountains, no valleys, a globe of prairies, flat and smooth as a billiard ball? No elephants, no mice, only dogs? Or, rather, elephants the size of dogs, mice the size of dogs? eagles the size of robins, hummingbirds the size of robins? Can we say that God wants no "heroes," no people filled with bread? no mothers of many? Surely we cannot. Nor do these words imply that every powerful person will suffer disabling reversal. The book Samuel shows that life's inequities persist, as the deaths of innocent people in 2 Sam 21:1-14 and 2 Sam 24 reveals.

We recall that the prayer celebrates God's holiness rather than his justice (see above p. 79), and assume that the negative reversals occur to people like those mentioned in v. 3. God wants no such powerful, rich, and many-sonned people who do not praise as Hannah does, who speak "so big, so big," who mouth arrogance (v. 3), who are enemies (v. 1) to God's faithful people, who are "adversaries" (v. 10) to God. Conversely, God wants stumblers who have put on divine strength, faithful hungry who are filled, and praying barren who become mothers many times over.

These are representative conditions having to do with physical strength, food, and family. In offering this prayer we assert that God regards the inequities which life presents, is not moved by power and other favourable circumstance, and retains ultimate and sovereign control over the lives of his people. Nothing in the NT asserts so strongly this vision of social order.

Once, while he was still at Cambridge, Solomon Schechter—later the founder of the Jewish Theological Seminary in New York—was asked by a friend, "Can you explain why, when I was a child, we were taught the OT in our Welsh schools, and when I visited Wales recently, there was a complete change, and the OT was replaced entirely by the New?" The scholar and rabbi answered, "Never mind, in times of stress, and when the world will be in need of moral strength, your schools will turn again to the OT."

In our world, so in need of moral strength, Hannah's prayer envisions the equitable order that God seeks and will finally have.

The use of passive or intransitive verbs in this section, however, leaves unexpressed the means by which such reversals may occur. I have already argued that the prayer gives us the voice of God's people looking to the future under priestly and prophetic leadership, that is to say, within the power of worship and preaching. It follows that the divine instruction (torah) and inspired proclamation (prophecy) are the primary means to accomplish the reversals which give God's people the level standing with one another which they already and always have with God. Torah can do this through its emphasis on fairness and social order (the laws which the biblical story associates with Sinai, for example, Exod 20-23; Lev 19; Deut 15:1-18). Prophecy does this through its unremitting call for moral integrity and equity.

Whereas scripture is written, prophecy is—in the first instance—spoken. Scripture is in a way institutional; prophecy is independent. Priest and prophet have sometimes been in tension or even conflict with one another, but in the biblical ideal the *prophet interprets the law that the priest teaches*. Written scripture is always there, but it is unchanging, inert and passive apart from understanding brought by the Spirit's illumination and needs to be matched by free-standing, interactive speech, speech that gives scripture the spin it needs for a concrete and particular occasion.

Luis Bunuel, the surrealist film-maker, once said the instruments of the orchestra had personalities. He called the piccolo "an ant's nest of sound;" the violin is the carpenter, contentedly sawing away. It is his view of the bass drum that interests me: "bold, prophetic, slightly rude."

God intends to address life's unfairness through prophetic speech, bold, and, with apologies, sometimes even slightly rude. Prophecy addresses God's people: it is through our obedience to the precepts of the covenant that God intends to effect whatever human equity is possible within the present order.

At the heart of the prayer, then, stands this vision of leveling: unasked, uncaused, unconditioned. This is the world which, in diaspora, God's people seek, under the nurturing power of divine worship and through obedience to torah and prophecy.

2. *God's action effects reversal* (vs. 6-8d)

The descriptive now gives way to the *confessional*. The concrete examples of circumstances in vs. 4-5, changed without agency or cause, now yield to direct assertion that God, acting in character, is One who affects human life most profoundly (vs 6-7), and especially One who reverses the condition of the poor and needy (v. 8a-d).

a. Contrasting divine actions (vs. 6-7)

All but one of the verbs in these four lines are in an elegant participial form. which indicates that God performs these actions. The emphasis falls on the divine character rather than the human situation. The LORD is the being who kills and makes alive. Behind the broken bow and the gift of manifold children is this divine Person.

Verse 6 asserts God's utter and absolute sovereignty over human existence.

Death and life are in his gift, as is also what lies beyond death. God has the power and the unconditional right to effect the reversals epitomized in vs. 4-5. We affirm this without denying the presence of secondary causation in life and death and without asserting that every act, especially of death, is God's direct will. "Sheol" is the shadowy land of the Old Testament's afterlife, inhabited by the dead, both good and bad.

This section has intimations about the future. The words "he brings up" translate the one verb in this sequence which is not a participle, even though I have translated it as if it were. It is a preterite, the normal form in narrative sequence, and by itself means, "he went up" or "he brought [someone] up." The MT has marked this verb as "unique" in the Bible, being spelled with a long "a" (*way-yāʿal*) instead of with a short "a" (*way-yaʿal*) as expected.

My interpretation is that the anomalous spelling is a hermeneutic signal, having to do with the resurrection of the dead. The conventional OT view is that people stay dead; if so, God does not, in fact, "bring up" as he brings down. We recall NT texts showing that in the time of Jesus and Paul there was conflict over the idea of resurrection. The prayer, then, rather than giving us the participle "brings up," which could be disputed, gives us "he brought/went up," and draws attention to it by spelling it slightly wrong and glossing it as unique.

To what does this point? I suggest that it points to a distinguished successor in Hannah's tradition, the prophet Elijah, who actually did go up into heaven. The event was future to Hannah but past to the reader of the larger biblical narrative, and the exact verb *way-yaʿal* is used of Elijah in 2 Kings 2:11. The translation of the prophet without seeing death and decay becomes an intimation of God's power to raise the dead.

Interpreted this way, the preterite verb shows an awareness of resurrection as an issue, one with which the MT is concerned and on which it even takes a position. Its intimation here sounds in the prayer an eschatological overtone.

Verse 7 moves into the human social world (compare vs. 4-5). There also it is God who acts to make drastic changes. He "impoverishes," as he did the Canaanite nations and as the prophet says God will do to Tyre (Zech 9:4), and "makes rich," as Saul promised to do for the one who killed Goliath (1 Sam 17:25). This leads to a general statement of abasement and elevation (v. 7), and then directly to v. 8 with its spectacular reversal of the lot of the poor and needy.

b. Elevation of the Poor and Needy (v. 8a-d)

The removal of the poor and needy from their misery is the single concrete instance of a reversal effected by God. Their degradation is expressed by sitting in the dust (compare Isa 47:1) and on heaps of refuse (Lam 4:5). This is not necessarily a metaphor, as Job sat in the ashes (Job 2:8) and outcast victims scavenge wherever they must (2 Kings 7:3). The lines in v. 8a-c are repeated in Ps 113:7-8a.

The positive reversal is that the LORD seats the poor and needy with nobility. This is the glad vision of rags-to-riches stories of every time and place. Here the negative reversal is not asserted (against v. 7); the nobles are still there, but the poor take their place among them. As a vision of an equitable social order, it is instructive to compare Psalm 113 at this point, which uses these same lines: "From the trash heaps God lifts the needy to seat them with nobles." Psalm 113 continues, "with the nobles of God's people," but Hannah's prayer takes a little different turn: "God grants them a throne of glory." The expression is lofty; it implies more than "a place of honor" and evokes the gathering of God's people in the age to come, when they will join Abraham and the others at table and will even reign with the Anointed One. Indeed, the reversal of positions of the rich man and Lazarus (Luke 16:19-31) is perfectly in keeping with Hannah's prayer, even to Jesus' insistence that "Moses and the prophets" are the means by which earth's people are to be awakened and turn to God (vs. 29-31) .

To recapitulate, the reversal of Hannah's barrenness is a magnificent gift of God's grace, which her prayer now projects onto the wider world and into the future. It stands for every reversal that God, by his people's obedience to torah and prophecy, accomplishes and intends to accomplish.

D. God's Continuing Triumph through His King (vs. 8e-10)

The voice of God's people celebrates the King to come. No statement of what human obedience can do is complete without recognizing its limits.There are limits both because of the intractable character of evil in our world and because of the frequent shortfall in our obedience. In exile God's people know with special clarity that the full perfection of our social relationships stands on the far side of events which we cannot ourselves bring about.

The last section of the prayer introduces the overt eschatological elements which vs. 6-8d have already intimated. It opens with a cosmological statement asserting God as the one who has founded the world itself. Linked to the preceding by "for," this justifies the claims of vs. 6-8d, since the one who put the very world in its place is surely also the sovereign of human existence. The God who is known at the prayer's opening as the Holy One who saves and protects us as people (vs. 1-2) is here the One who already created the world's ordered existence. It also justifies the claims of vs 9-10 that God will deal decisively against the powers of evil in the world, since the founder of the world, present in primeval time, is also the world's judge.

Those who talk "so big, so big" (v. 3) will finally be silenced (v. 9b). They are "the wicked" and that they are to be silenced "in darkness" moves us away from the present moment to what follows. For God to "guard the feet of his faithful" will have the same range of meaning: God protects his faithful as they walk and will see them safely through life's trials. The verb "prevail" gives a verbal link with the *gibbôrîm* "heroes" whose bow God breaks and with the other negative reversals above (vs. 4-5).

The finest "human strength" will not avail in the end (v. 9c). This is the warning of all scripture—law, prophets, and writings—using the same language as Hannah's prayer. For example, in the torah Lev. 26:20 asserts, "Your *kōăḥ* will be spent to no purpose." In the prophets Amos 2:14 declares, "The strong will find no *kōăḥ*, and the *gibbôr* will not save his life," and in the writings Ps. 33:16 expresses the same theology. "The king is not saved by great might; the *gibbôr* is not rescued by great *kōăḥ*." Samson's *kōăḥ* did not avail, apart from obedience, nor did Saul's. Insofar as God's people "prevail" in the present, it is a gift of God's miraculous power, and earth's Founder guarantees that the story will end right.

Those who were our "enemies" in v. 1 are here God's "adversaries" (v. 10a), part of the prayer's move to see one's concrete historical struggle and its resolution as an instance of God's ongoing struggle with evil. Without patient humility, the equation could become arrogant, but the idea is thoroughly biblical.

Not only so, behind the many contenders against God's will in the world, there is a single embodiment of hostility (v. 10a-b, see the discussion above of v. 3). The text shows us this by preserving, beside the plural "adversaries," a second tradition of reading the text as "his adversary." The plural "adversaries" agrees with the verb "they will be shattered," but the singular "adversary" agrees with "against him" in the next line. By preserving both readings, the MT refers once again to the dark figure of the anti-messiah, that larger-than-life embodiment of evil who surfaces again and again in human history.

In exile God's people hope for the King to come, knowing all too well that even now his opposite may be at work, resisting all that God's holiness requires.

In the last days of the Ceaucescu regime in Romania, underground humor circulated a story about a man who each day eagerly scanned the front page of the newspaper. His wife finally asked him what he was looking for. "The obituaries," he said. She replied, "The obituaries are never on the front page." He said, "The one I'm looking for will be!" When Ceaucescu was finally dead, western news media reported that the Romanians said, "The antichrist died on Christmas day!"

The anti-messiah begins to loom in the future almost as soon as messianic hope arises, and his presence in Hannah's prayer alongside the King to come is a mark of the prayer's eschatological reference.

The adversaries shattered, thunder resounding against the rival, "the LORD judges the ends of the earth" (v. 10c-e). The words imply universal rule, fair and equitable, administered by God's anointed King to whom all strength and confidence belong. The verbs "he will give" and "he will lift" are in a form which suggests that they follow as a result from the LORD'S judging the ends of the earth. In this eschatology the rule of the King *follows upon* God's judging the ends of the earth.

It is obvious to the reader of the Hannah-and-Samuel story that Israel has no king. The complex forces which led to the rise of kingship have yet to take place. Although her son will play a major role in these developments, Hannah's prayer is not about Israel's king, but God's. We see the difference clearly when we compare the Greek text, which reads, "He gives strength to our kings"—not "his king," but "our kings." The plural can refer only to the sequence of human kings yet to come as Hannah speaks. The singular "his king" opens allusively to the future of God's people under the King to come. Coming at the end of the prayer, following defeat of the enemies/enemy, this vision clearly belongs to Israel's hope for a glorious future in the days of the Messiah. Then and then only will life's inequities be fully reversed.

The Toronto "Globe and Mail" carries a daily quote for its readers under the caption "Thought du jour." In one of them it offered us the wisdom of one Spider Robinson, an American-born science fiction writer who was denied permanent entry into Canada until 1976 because, as he says, "the Canadian immigration officials in New York didn't have any such occupation as science-fiction writer." The proffered wisdom is this: "Science fiction is the only genre I've discovered which assumes there's going to be a future."

Spider should read the Bible. Its prophetic voice, raised in 1 Sam 2:1-10 in declaratory prayer, has never doubted it. "The bows of heroes are broken, the faltering have belted on strength.... The LORD will judge the ends of the earth, and so gives strength to his king and lifts the head of his anointed."

Thanks be to God!

THE TRANSFIGURATION OF POWER

RICHARD W. CARLSON

This essay has its genesis in stories, particularly those of people who have been subject to the abuse and misuse of power within the church. To protect the privacy of their pain and to insure the anonymity of those who have hurt them, the stories will inform but not be told. What is public is the response occasioned in me and here directed to the church.

WHAT THE CHURCH IS TO BE

The church and its prefiguring in the people of God of the Hebrew Bible is a complex and multifaceted institution or organism. In the NT alone there are over ninety images or metaphors to describe the church.[1] Its richness extends beyond picture to purpose. It is to be many things:

> The church is to be a body called and gifted for mission, expansion, and witness. (Matt 28:19-20; Acts 1:8; Isa 60:1-3; 2 Cor 5:18-20)
>
> The church is to be a gathering for worship and praise. (Pss 8:2, 33:1, 66:8, 68:19, 100:1-5; Rom 12:1; Heb 13:15)
>
> The church is to be a place of nurture, encouragement, and care. (Deut 4:9-10; 10:12-19; John 13:14-17, 34-35; Acts 4:32-35; Rom 12:9-13, 15:7; Eph 4:32-5:2; 1 Thess 4:18)
>
> The church is to be in process of being built up and growing. (Ps 127:1, John 15:5ff; 1 Cor 14:12; Eph 4:12-16; 1 Thess 5:11)
>
> The church is to be a people especially chosen and set apart. (Exod 19:5-6; Isa 62:12; Eph 1:11ff.; 1 Pet 2:4-10)
>
> The church is to be a place where authority in God's name is to be employed and exercised. (Isa 61:1-3; Matt 16:18-19).

Beyond these half dozen teleological "marks" of the church there are surely several more. But for this paper's focus we must mention but one other.

> The church is to be a sanctuary, a place of safety (2 Sam. 7:10-11; Ps 100:3; John 17:11-12a). It is a safe place where alien and sojourner can find refuge and share in common rights (Exod 23:9; Num 15:15). It is a sheepfold guarded by a good shepherd (John 10:11-16), and when threatened by the faithlessness of its other guardians, it becomes the object of God's own shepherding (Ezek 34:25-31). As representative of its Creator, the church is a haven of protective wings (Ps 91:4; Luke 13:34) for vulnerable creatures.

VICTIMIZATION AND SURVIVAL

When God's creatures find themselves becoming victim to the misuse of power in the very place which is both named sanctuary and known for its safety, in a place offering faith, hope, and love, those wounded experience more than disillusionment. For most of them, if not all, what has been lost was not an illusion. The loss of confidence in a safe place, which they still want to be very real, can lead them in reflexive mode to begin to blame themselves for whatever acts and consequences cluster around the misuse of power. Such is the nature of victimization. Such people drown in an overflow of insecurity. For those who refuse to remain victims, for those who fight back and focus their anger on the proponents or systems of abusive power, for those who care for their yet God-created selves, there is hope for survival.

Only those who would profit by victimization would not want all victims to walk the courageous road to survival. But even if all who have been hurt within the context of sanctuary were to survive, full celebration is not in order unless one can celebrate such testimony as "I (We) survived the church." Lest power continue to be misused, some address must be given to the church.

This essay will explore the taxonomy of power and how it might be recast. Some suggestions for the amendment of ecclesial life will be followed by a liturgical conclusion.

THE PEOPLE BEHIND THE STORIES

But first let be named, by category, those whose stories are the energy behind this exploration. Some of the stories of victimization have been told by those who have been abused or otherwise hurt simply because of their givenness in creation. They were born female or Afro-American.

Other stories have been told about events that happened to them in time and in the context of the church. These are persons sexually abused as children, as teenagers, or as adults; or they are those sexually harassed in their ecclesiastical workplace.

Third are the stories of those painfully caught in a lack of cultural consensus. These are gay men and lesbians who are societally and religiously hurt because they fail to fit the norm, or they bend the pattern, break the common sense, or offend the consciousness. Regardless of the position one takes on this subject, the church must be sensitive to the isolation, pressure, and dilemma these people feel.[2]

All the above are more than categories.[3] They are numerous persons who in their uniqueness and category are not me. Therefore I do not pretend to represent them. Nor do I pretend that they are representative of a common fabric among themselves.[4] Pain can be common but it is always particular and experienced uniquely.

The focus here is not to respond to the stories but to address the church in which the pain was occasioned and in which I have long held privilege, position, and power and which I now by this essay hope to continue to serve faithfully.

THE NATURE OF POWER

Fundamentally, the phenomenon of power is the ability of an individual or collectivity to do something, to have the capacity to act. As Emily Dickinson has simply put it: "To be alive is Power, existence in itself, without a further function, omnipotence enough."[5] Were we yet in Eden or at the end of time in the kingdom such would be sufficient. But in the mean time power assumes a more interactive character to both benevolent and malevolent ends. In the latter case, power is the ability to act upon or over against others. It is the ability to control, influence, sway, or compel others. As Max Weber states, "By power is meant that opportunity existing within a social relationship which permits one to carry out one's own will even against resistance and regardless of the basis on which this opportunity rests."[6]

Like the church, power is a complex and multifaceted phenomenon, complicated in its categorization by nuances of meaning in different contexts. Besides Weber, persons like Rollo May, psychoanalyst, and John Kenneth Galbraith, economist, have recently attempted to provide taxonomies for understanding power.[7] A variation of May's structuring will be accepted in this paper.

In any classification of the types of power, attention is given to its correlate, authority. Most often authority is subsumed as a secondary type, but there are some crucial linguistic differences. In both Greek and Latin, "power" *(dunamis, potestas)* carries connotations of ability or capability owned or seized by one. "Authority" (*exousia, auctoritas*) literally is in a process, emerging out-of-being, neither bestowable nor produced, but earned over time.

> Authority is distinctive in that it is based not on position but conviction. It is not institutionally but personally related.... one can say that *auctoritas* does not rest upon the attributes and capabilities.... but upon the recognition of these by others.... only in the fact that people agree with an authority, follow it, and submit to it does this authority actually emerge. From this it also follows that in principal *potestas* has to do with compulsion, while *auctoritas* always has to do with freedom.[8]

That Jesus taught with *exousia,* not as the teachers of the law (Matt 7:28), was the witness of the crowd in response to his person rather than to his exercise of power. Similarly a church leader with "authority" is one who "over time" has earned the respect, trust, and confidence of the people he/she serves and leads. If that trust is broken, it is because authority is forfeited in the seizing and misusing of power. If authority is at all to be classified as a subset of power, it may be called *"referent* power," the extent to which persons feel closeness to and identification with another in leadership. As such it might be part of the dynamics involved in the fourth and fifth types of power discussed below.

Lord Acton's famous nineteenth century dictum, "Power corrupts and absolute power corrupts absolutely" best refers to the first of May's types, *exploitative* power.[9] This kind of power, rooted in a hierarchical world-view, is the most destructive kind of power in that it is the ability to subject persons to whatever use they may have to the one who holds the power. Slavery is an obvious example. This kind of power always presupposes violence or threat of violence on those who, as its victims, have neither choice nor freedom. Exploitative power justifies itself either on the basis of a greater good maintenance of order, or on the notion that some people (those in power) are endowed with clearer vision or divine right to claim the importance of their action (or belief) as greater than the people who are crushed under its weight. Rewards and punishments doled out or demanded by those in power are common expressions of this type and are used to maintain control.

The second type of power, the *manipulative,* is illustrated on our own frontier by the superseding of the gunman by the con-man. This is still power *over* persons, but it uses indirect control to manage people. To manipulate effectively, those who exercise this kind of power must directly control phenomena such as information, access, and norms.

Part of the control of information is the creation of an ideology which filters any-fresh, or oppositional, data. Strong efforts to influence the dominance and meanings of certain images are coupled with apparent open sharing of information, but in reality, not all of it. In its severest form this becomes propaganda, presenting only one form of reality while attacking any other representation.

Access has to do with tokenism, or the disproportionate representation of the powerless. Through co-optation and seemingly benevolent rewards, tokenism controls access to power by so manipulating reality as to make it look like something it is not. A few "outsiders" get taken into the center of the system in order to keep the rest quietly outside the gates.

Even Weber typified this form of power as "legitimate." But its legitimacy rests on those in power controlling a group's or society's norms. Broadly speaking, norms are "what the rules are here," both written and unwritten, both conceptual and behavioral. In order for manipulative power to be legitimated, it must control laws, traditions, customs, and standards by which knowledge is evaluated and obtained. It also seeks to control the *perceptions* of potential rewards and punishments, mattering not whether in fact these exist. Power over these phenomena yields perceptions among the people or the powerless that see only one side of the world. Moreover, as Joan Chittister argues, "Since the community supports the powerful, therefore the onus for nonconformity will fall on the follower who resists the system."[10] It is a painful irony that the conditions whereby a people freely grant authority to a leader are a manipulation of the very minds of the people themselves. Again Chittister:

> Since the legitimacy of power rests in the minds of the masses, not in the inherency of the powerful, manipulation is the key to being able to maintain a system, where people are made to be less than they can be.[11]

Of course they do not realize, what has been done to them.

A third form of power, the *competitive* is more egalitarian. It is still "us and them" but the "them" has a fighting chance. This type of power is power *against*. It is win-lose, and it is based on a world-view wherein "nobody remembers who came in second," or as novelist Gore Vidal has cynically observed about the temper of our times: "It is not enough to succeed; others must fail." The basic structure of competitive power is the team mentality. As such it can provide zest and vitality to human relations but its drawbacks are inordinately severe.

Competitive power assumes that some people by nature are better than others and that, whatever the rhetoric of equality, power is not meant to be shared. Ultimately this form of power becomes increasingly parochial; it shrinks the area of community in which one lives because any alternative person, grouping, or form of power must be defeated. Furthermore, this form of power can become insidious when, not only seeking to win, it reverses the field and denies the other the right to play the game at all.

More positive than the above is a fourth type of power, the *nutrient* (nurturant), which is power *for* the other. Its best example, which reveals its potential for ill as well as for good is the parental exercise of power for the vulnerable child. Where its goal may not be to make others dependent, if it continues over time without nurturant effect, e.g., the independence of the other, it becomes paternalistic (maternalistic) and its object becomes indebted. It is based on an "idealism" that is twofold: 1) that if people are enabled to develop, they will, and be of benefit to all; and 2) "the notion that all things are created good and that all things bear within them a spark of the divine."[12] As such, grounded in Genesis 1 and 2, it begs the question of the meaning of Genesis 3 and, in hope, can overlook the reality of the experience of victims in the mean time.

The final type of power May calls the *integrative.* It is one person or group acting powerfully *with* another, a power that is devoted to mutual concern and the development of both parties. Chittister describes it as follows:

> Integrative power is power used to bring unlike needs into unity. It synthesizes the needs of both parties into one organic whole. It sets out. . . .to empower. . . to create a world where relationships are formed out of both need and gift and no one is expected to lose.[13]

Citing the peace and civil rights movements as examples of integrative power, both May and Chittister argue that it requires a kind of innocence which does not renounce responsibility nor tries to gain anything for the self, but focuses on the community and structures of collaboration. Contemporary examples of this within the black community are pointed to by Cornel West who compares both Martin Luther King, Jr. and Malcolm X with most present black political leaders who "appear too hungry for status to be angry, too eager for acceptance to be bold, too self-invested to be defiant. . . . whose bold rhetoric is more performance than personal, more play-acting than heartfelt."[14] That this could characterize contemporary leadership in many other communities and quarters, including the ministerium of which this writer is a member, must be said lest we identify a black issue as uniquely theirs.

West goes on to give more substance to the "innocence" mentioned above as characteristic of those who exemplify the use of integrative power. He employs the term "humility" for it.

> Similarly Malcolm, Martin. . . were examples of humility. . . even Malcolm's aggressiveness was accompanied by a common touch and humble disposition toward ordinary black people. Humility is the fruit of inner security and wise maturity. To be humble is to be so sure of one's self and one's mission that one can forego calling excessive attention to one's self and status. And even more pointedly, to be humble is to revel in the accomplishments or potentials of others.[15]

This is the essence of integrative power.

In concluding this taxonomic section, it is important to note May's warning to anyone so caught in self-righteous rigidity as to claim immunity from any one or all forms of power. These five kinds of power can be "all present in the same person (or collectivity) at different times. . . The question—and it is a moral one—is the proportion of each kind in the total spectrum."[16]

THE MISUSE AND ABUSE OF POWER

Often in church systems any misuse or abuse of power occasions intense focus on the particularities of specific actions and on the persons involved, though more on the perpetrator than on the victim. Such focus, while understandable, is myopic in ignoring that misuse of power always happens in a larger context. In her discussion of professional ethics, especially of the clergy, Karen Lebacqz, following Berger-Luckman, argues:

> The question is not simply whether the individual practitioner abuses the

> individual client. The question is also whether the social construction of reality provided by the profession is one that adequately reflects the needs and interests of society, or whether it perpetuates biases and unjust structures.[17]

Thus the character of the dominant world-view or ideology within the context can determine whether a particular act is indeed a misuse of power or not. If there is common acceptance of the hierarchial world in which exploitative power flourishes or the Manichean playing field as the real world on which competitive power struggles, then winning at all costs or suppression of all challenge is not misuse of power, but its proper exercise. Therefore the ideological components that are normative in these constructed realities are equally critical. Predominantly in the west and in the church these components include the following: patriarchy, white supremacy, heterosexual exclusivity, and an understanding of sexuality as more functional than relational. Regrettably all too often these same ideological themes are woven together in the unspoken but ever-present tapestry behind the stage on which manipulative power is played out.

Over against the first three forms of power, this paper takes the position that in whatever name, by whatever doctrine, or to whatever end, the abuse and misuse of power is any activity that depends on overpowering, however flagrant or subtle, for its result. May two examples illustrate:

1. Sadly, the fear of the fiscal consequences of litigation, more than concern for the discipline of the perpetrators or justice for their victims, has driven the abuse of power in sexual exploitation to front page notoriety. Sexual exploitation has become a priority issue for the church and other professional bureaucracies. Clergy failure to acknowledge the power gap between professional and client and live up to professional standards increases vulnerability of the abused and shatters images of those who were trusted to heal, to represent, and to bear grace.[18] That sexual exploitation is carried on by ecclesiastical lay leaders, as well as the professional clergy, is, in the experience of the writer, a phenomenon increasingly named and addressed. The "power gap" may not be as great, but the ideological backdrop remains the same in these cases.

2. A second kind of example cuts across all categories of the misuse of power, whether the "victims" be women, people of color, or gay men and lesbians. This is the phenomenon of "blaming the victim," a phrase which is the title of William Ryan's classic dissection of racism in America.[19] Albert Bandura observes that:

> When bad practices are well entrenched, efforts on the part of concerned individuals to halt them by publicizing their destructive effects are more likely to arouse derogation than sympathy for the victims.... It is easier to reduce the discomfort by designating the victims as a bad person than to challenge bad practices that are an accepted part of the social order.[20]

West argues that the spectrum of views of race on the American landscape shares the common denominator that black people are "problem people."[21] The blame is inherent in and on them. For gay men and lesbians the message is the same. Scanzoni and Mollenkott quote a letter written to an evangelical Christian magazine:

> Less than two months ago I was told by a sincere Christian counselor that it would be "better to repent and die," even if I had to kill myself, than to go on living and relating to others as a homosexual. (A friend of mine, who

> was told something similar by a well-intentioned priest, did just that.)[22]

Surely this kind of insensitivity cannot be tolerated in the church.

POWER IN THE BIBLE

In the Bible the agents who exercise power are many but the source of power ultimately is one. Human beings exercise the power of choice and free will, but this is a result of being made in God's image (Gen 1:27-28). Kings, priests, prophets, chieftains, family fathers, all political leaders of any kind exercise their power as they will. But it always has a religious base: such power is from God and they are accountable to God for this use. Even the ecclesial power given to the Apostle Peter (Matt 16:18-19) in the form of the keys are but symbolic of the rule and authority of their real holder, Jesus (Rev 3:7). The same holds true for the powers of binding and loosing given to all the Apostles (Matt 18:18; John 20:23). Such powers are from Christ and persons exercising them are accountable to Christ. To be sure, there are powers also present in evil spirits who in NT times are under obeisance to Satan. But such concentration of oppositional power is ultimately to be overcome by the power of God who from creation to consummation exercises providential power in time.

Even though the wisdom tradition locates power directly in the grasp of the human creature by dint of wisdom and care (cf. Prov 3:27; 24:5) the overall thematic of the scriptures may be found in the *texti classici*, " 'Not by might, nor by power, but by my Spirit,' says the Lord of hosts" (Zech 4:6) and "We have this treasure in earthen jars to show that this all-surpassing power is from God and not from us" (2 Cor 4:7).

These texts stand as affirmation of God as the source of power and as an implicit warning of the use of power for anything other than God's purposes. "When we forget the sources of that power, use it for selfish reasons, claim credit for its effects (Deut 8:17-18) or misdirect it away from God's intent, then we have misused power.[23]

There is another dimension of God's power in the Bible that exhibits God's display of power in uncommon ways (1 Cor 1:27-29). Janet Lundblad has written,

> The Bible speaks of a God who hides power in most inauspicious individuals and settings: a young shepherd holding a slingshot, a beautiful Jewess bowing low before the outstretched scepter of an oriental King, a carpenter and his young wife guarding their newly-born baby, a Nazarene rabbi hanging on a cross, executed as a criminal.[24]

It is particularly the person of Jesus whose own response to power is "an embarrassment when measured against our most widely approved standards of behavior." Lloyd J. Averill goes on to say:

> I simply cannot fathom his refusal to exert the power that was within his reach when it is clear that power was the only language his enemies could have understood.... It is precisely what we have done, over and over again. . . . Urged again and again to resort to the kind of power against men and women that depends on overpowering, he refused.[25]

As Paul Lehman has suggested, "the *ultima ratio* of submission and silence is their power to expose the weakness of power before the power of weakness."[26]

In the third temptation in the wilderness (Matt 4:8ff), as well as on the cross, Jesus refused to be captured by the lure of power. Henri Nouwen, writing on a contemporary temptation for church leaders to desire to lead rather than be led (cf. John 21:18), argues that the temptation to power is seemingly irresistible because

> . . . power offers an easy substitute for the hard task of love. It seems easier to be God than to love God, easier to control people than to love people, easier to own life than to love life.... The long, painful history of the Church is the history of people ever and again tempted to choose power over love, control over the cross, being a leader over being led.[27]

Jesus displayed power as he proclaimed the rule of God over humanity and the love of God for humankind. In word and deed he also demonstrated God's will for new life, meaningful and whole, and thus in God's power he stands "in irreconcilable opposition to every metaphysical glorification of human political powers, and in the same way to the claim of a theocracy that by appeal to God's lordship wants only to press its own demand for power."[28]

Finally, on the cross Jesus' suffering becomes a sign of God's solidarity with the powerless in their own suffering and thus offers to those victimized by power a paradox of promise beyond survival itself

THE ONTOLOGY AND ETHICS OF POWER

It is sometimes helpful in attempting to discern the nature of a phenomenon to examine it not in isolation but in relation. For example, the nature of human anger in its aggressive expression is not only better understood when related to the dynamics of submissiveness and assertiveness, but options for its amelioration are presented as well.[29] It is similarly so with the phenomenon of power, which when left to be explored alone, leaves one with either-or choices rather than any creative synergy which may not only illumine but prescribe.

Therefore we turn now to a singular work of a complex theologian, Paul Tillich, specifically his lectures on love, power, and justice, appropriately delivered three times in different places before being gathered in one volume.[30] Tillich's concern in this work is twofold: 1) the ethical concern is to bring balance and realistic meaning in human life to the three terms of the title, and 2) this is built on an ontological analysis of how love, power, and justice are related in being (God) itself. If Tillich's treatment is not classically trinitarian, it is at least co-relationally triadic.

It is beyond my present purpose (and capability) to attempt to give a synopsis of Tillich's argument, but I would suggest that its genius is in its very triadic arrangement. That the being of God, or the structures of everything that participates in being, is constituted by love, power, and justice provides expanded interpretation to the nature of the *imago dei* and insight into how power might function in human life. As Tillich claims,

> Justice, power, and love towards oneself is rooted in the justice, power and love which we receive from that which transcends us and affirms us. The relation to ourselves is a function of our relation to God.[31]

It might be helpful to picture the elements of love, power, and justice as the three points of an equilateral triangle whose center is human unity both individually and corporately. In the model, arrows point in both directions along all three sides indicating dynamic influence at all times in all directions. Thus if an individual or a group is denied justice, or receives but partial justice, love and power are adversely affected as well. Love, which is fundamentally constitutive of identity, is eroded by any fracture of justice or the organizational arrangements in which one lives and works.[32] To deny one justice is to send as well a message about the diminishing of one's worth. Similarly, in the absence of equal justice, one's power or ability to act is likewise constrained. Full freedom both to be (love) and to do (power) is truncated in any system where organizational arrangements (justice) are biased against a particular person or group. Thus in the middle to late sixties, during the time of the civil rights movement, not only was justice needed to address legislative matters and court enforcement, the people oppressed for so long had to address as well the elements of love and power. Therefore the cry came not only for "black power" both in thoughtful articulation and its enraged expression, but also for the self-affirmation of a people ("black is beautiful") and their culture in an attempt to reclaim an identity buried under years of slavery and multiple forms of segregation. Regrettably, as Cornell West argues in his book *Race Matters*, issues of full expression of love, power, and justice are still paramount thirty years later:

> Only if we are willing to grow and confront the new challenges posed by the black rage of our day will we take the black freedom struggle to a new and higher level. The future of this country may well depend on it.[33]

Without intending to trivialize the black experience, another example on a more personal level might further illustrate the dynamics of the model. There are many Christians who have come to a vibrant faith in the love of God and who have been promised in the organizational arrangements of their communities that they are free, in fact encouraged, to express that faith in witness and praise. Then, when in the power of the Spirit they begin to demonstrate charismatic activity, many find their power to act constrained by strong liturgical norms. Often sanctions follow which leave these now-thwarted faithful either disgruntled with the structures or doubtful of themselves. This dynamic happens in churches, not just over charismatic expression, but to children, youth, women, the elderly, the divorced, the sexually wounded, people of color, those of alternative sexual orientation, and so they are left confirmed in powerlessness, wondering about their worth and distrustful of the system.

Or love itself may be the point of the triangle under attack. A person or group may be promised full justice and freedom to act, but if their selfhood and identity are under constant attack and ridicule, a resultant lack of self-worth evaporates any desire to act at all. Even just processes and guarantees fail to address the problem. Cartesian dualisms are more than philosophical points of argument. They hide the painful fractioning of human life which promises hope to the half or one-third whole untouched by pain, but ignore the comprehensive destruction.

At the risk of getting stuck in a Reformation/Calvinistic/Barthian framework, let me suggest that the fundamental triad of doctrines of the Christian life (justification, sanctification and vocation) and the character of the Holy Trinity are at work in this model as well. The redeeming love of God, supremely expressed in Jesus the Christ, is the basis for justification and confirms the worth and identity of each person. The comforting and challenging power of the Spirit equips, encourages, and enables people to act and to grow in grace (sanctification). And the commending Creator gives stewarding vocation to humankind to tend the earth and the relationships of all its creatures so that justice might obtain for all.

This is not at all to suggest that the issue of power is thereby spiritualized into devotional exercises and anxious sorting out of who has which gift and whether the fruit (Gal 5:22f) is ripe. The black experience alone guards against such reductionism. As West argues, a "pervasive spiritual impoverishment" is at the heart of the "social deracination and cultural denudement" of black urban dwellers.[34] So if not spiritualized, power must be seen as having to do with the spirit and never separated from issues of love and justice. As Rollo May states, "work for justice would not be possible without a combination of power and love."[35]

AN ADDITIONAL TRIAD FROM SCRIPTURE

An eighth century (B.C.E.) prophet, Micah of Moresheth, provides further triadic illumination towards an analysis of power. Like his contemporaries, Amos and Hosea in Israel and Isaiah in Jerusalem, Micah was deeply distressed by the injustice and corruption he witnessed around him. Bribery (3:11), dishonesty (6:10-11), distrust that destroyed families (7:5-6), and silent clergy concerned only with their own well-being (3:5,11) did not prevent Micah from having a hope for light beyond darkness (7:8) because of a majestic God who was over all events. Micah believed that there would come a time when all people oppressed by those who carry out evil simply because they have the power to do it (2:1) would at last find safety and sanctuary (4:4).

Like several other prophets, Micah in his sixth chapter employs the metaphor of a heavenly law court. Though the case is against Israel, the implications are clear for Judah as well. Central to the trial is Micah's response to the defendants' plea of coming with offerings as part of a sacrificial system of atonement. Like Jesus who spoke woe to the hypocrites who offered their tithes but neglected the weightier matters of the law (Matt 23:23), Micah states in language that is a focal summary of prophetic faith, hope, and challenge:

> This is what Yahweh asks of you:
> only this, to act justly,
> to love tenderly, and to walk humbly with your God.
> (Micah 6:8, Jerusalem Bible)

As Juan I. Alfaro comments on this scene:

> God does not want more victims. God hates the very idea of human victims of any kind. God does not want sacrifices except the sacrifice of self through the life of justice, so that no person will be sacrificed or victimized. . . . God wants service expressed principally in the practice of love and justice.[36]

Thus synthesizing the prophecies of Amos (justice over sacrifice), Hosea (the importance of tenderness and love), and Isaiah (faith and obedience to God), Micah presents a triad of what life is to be for the individual, for Israel, for Judah, and by extension for the church. The first two commands are fairly straightforward. But justice is more than simply following social and religious obligations. "It implies a commitment and a responsibility for the defense of the poor and the powerless so that they will not be victimized by the more powerful."[37] Loving mercy is likewise more than human feelings; it includes compassion for and solidarity with those unprotected and in need.[38]

At issue is the meaning of "walking humbly with God." If two-thirds of Micah's call is in parallel with love and justice, how might walking humbly further inform our understanding of power?

Both Alfaro and Wolf contend that "walking humbly" has a distinct dimension of attentiveness, thoughtfulness, and watchfulness. It suggests a focus away from self to listening both to the heart of God and the cries of the poor and dispossessed and to seeing things and events through God's eyes. This consonance with the themes of love and justice can, however, obscure the fact that humility here is not to be interpreted as self-abnegation. It is not "an ethical posture of being ready to accept a lower social ranking... or any false posture of submission... but instead points to a driving force that makes it even possible for persons to foster new community and to direct their will according to God's deeds and commands."[39] Thus, while surely warning against pride and arrogance (Prov 11:2; Jas 4:6), to "walk humbly with God" has about it a purposefulness and dignity, precisely because the one who walks humbly walks with God and towards God's intent. The self is not subsumed but ennobled, the walking is not a submissive shuffle but a confident stride.

Because of its linkage with justice and love, "walking humbly" at once both approximates power and transfigures it. As Walter Brueggemann says:

> To do justice, to love kindness, to walk humbly with God—these may embody all that we need to know in order to be faithful and to be human. They are not three virtues or "things to do"... rather they speak of three dimensions of a life of faithfulness, each of which depends on and is reinforced by the other two.[40]

As Cornel West described the "humility" of Martin Luther King, Jr. and Malcolm X having to do with inner security, wise maturity, and missional clarity,[41] so the humility called for by Micah reflects as much the wisdom/creation tradition of scripture as it avoids excessive self-negation in the fall/redemption paradigms which tend to dominate most of western, and especially evangelical, theology. Again Brueggemann writes:

> Wisdom theology treats man like a king: valued, powerful, and free if he is to accept the responsibility wisdom places upon him to choose life for himself and his fellows... wisdom theology makes sense only with people who love self enough to care and to celebrate....too much our theology is grounded in self-hate.[42]

The root word for humility in Latin is *humus*, meaning earth, soil, dirt. Because the Bible is set in a primarily agrarian, pastoral, or rural landscape, and because its metaphors are often organic, it has much to say about dirt, earth, and clay. Who we are is from clay (Gen 2:7) or the grass that grows from it (Isa 40:6; 1 Pet 1:24). We are the clay that the divine potter fashions into usefulness and purpose (Jer 18:1-6). As mentioned earlier we singly and collectively are clay vessels to hold the treasure of the gospel (2 Cor 4:7). We are the soils in or onto which the seed of salvation is cast (Matt 13:18-23).

There is a way of regarding the earthiness of human nature as denigration and ground for our self-hate. So the suitor, Sergius, attempts to defame the servant Louka in G. B. Shaw's, *Arms and the Man*: "... you are an abominable little clod of common clay, with the soul of a servant." But Louka, in name of that dignity which is hers in being equally created with this powerful military officer, responds: "You know how to hurt with your tongue as well as with your hands. But I don't care. . . whatever clay I'm made of, you're made of the same."

To acknowledge our finitude in humility need not be to assume our unworthiness. In fact to embrace finitude is both the ground of creation and its promise. It is to recognize limits or boundaries which can be taken either as defining or confining. When seen as the latter, they are boundaries to be broken, and the misuse of power is the agency by which they are transgressed. To see them rather as defining is to acknowledge the created dignity in the other. Moreover the limits of created creatureliness are not to be viewed as condemnation but as an object of celebration. Those limits are vast and "crowned with glory and honor" (Ps 8:4-8).

In the decade I have been teaching conflict management I have experienced that all too many of us come to personal or ecclesiastical struggles with dispositions towards submissiveness and self-blame until the suppressed anger festers too long or the pain reaches a point beyond bearing so that aggression (power over) takes control. More than simply a self-help growth skill, learning the option of assertiveness is at the heart of healthy humility and wisdom and the nexus of love, power, and justice in human exchange. To quote David Augsburger:

> The assertive lifestyle recognizes that loveless power violates, powerless love abdicates, but power and love in balance create justice. Justice is the arithmetic of love that works out the fair and equal distribution of power. True power is not power over but power to. Power is the ability to be self-affirming in spite of internal tension and external negation. Power is the energy to be other-affirming as well, to live justly in equal respect for others, and to love justly in equal regard for each person's worth.[43]

According to Cornel West, because "the crisis in black America is twofold: too-much poverty and too little self-love," we must adopt a new agenda for life lived together—"the frank acknowledgement of the basic humanness of all of us."[44] Might not this begin in humble listening to the assertive, creation-affirming, powerful witness of those who have been misused by the power of others?

QUESTIONS FOR AMENDMENT OF ECCLESIAL LIFE

Because the issues surrounding the abuse/misuse of power in the church are so multiple and complex, I have chosen to raise questions rather than give directions. The particularity of individual perspective cannot pretend to voice the mandate. Rather these issues invite collegial deliberation and collective response. The questions are gathered under three broad categories: theological education, church systems (both national and local), and the character of theological paradigms that affect personal and public spirituality.

1. *Theological education*

- To what degree does the nature of most theological education reinforce competitive power as a primary mode of learning by its emphasis on individual performance and achievement?
- In what ways is the examination of power and its abuse/misuse at all a focus in the curriculum?

• How does the seminary experience cultivate a healthy humility, a self-affirming creatureliness coupled with a vision for the unity of humankind made hopeful by education in skills for justice-making and peace-keeping?

• In what ways do models for integrative learning across disciplines provide alternatives to power struggles for "turf" control among faculties?

• As servant of the church, how does a seminary provide a context of safety for those who bring to it stories of the abuse of power in their lives so that they might both speak their story and find full security in processes governing student life.

2. *The Church*

• What kinds of education are provided for congregations regarding issues of abuse and which seek to insure safety and, at least, proximate justice for those who are objects of misuse of power?

• How might the church protect itself from becoming victim to the image-marketing of the prevailing and powerful culture which, by its emphases on *achievement, affluence,* and *appearance,* creates "victims" by the millions of those who have no chance of playing the game at all, much less winning it?[45]

How might the church begin to model patterns of integrative power in leadership styles, in committees, and in modes of interaction?

• Is the resurgence of the oppositional and militaristic, at least in metaphor, in the worship of the church more a sign of the paranoia of those who feel a loss of power than a witness of those who are truly persecuted for the integrity of their faith? If so how might this be addressed?

3. *Theology and spirituality*

• Do we need to return to an earlier decade and include in discipleship training and spiritual formation/direction some skill development in assertiveness as an option over against powerful aggression or victimized submission?

• Is basic human intimacy the issue? Are we a people whose tremulous hold on self-worth or timid fear of boundary breaking/reaching causes us as Nouwen suggests, to grab at power and control because "intimacy itself is a threat?"[46]

• Does the dominant western emphasis on the forensic (Anselmian) metaphors for the atonement so focus the nature of sin in terms of guilt, punishment, forgiveness, and acquittal that in issues of the abuse of power attention is naturally centered on its progenitor and not on those affected?

• Does not the effect of the misuse of power in the church on the wounded call for a more comprehensive theological treatment of the dynamics of shame and consequent metaphors of outcast, aloneness, reputation, return, and welcome? What theology of the atonement can address this?[47]

• Finally, how can the mandate for justice be synchronized with a mercy that "triumphs over judgment" (Jas 2:13)? Is it a matter of rhetoric over time that finally sacrifices the victim in the name of a higher righteousness? Or is it, if not in the vindication of the oppressed, a passion which embraces all persons in a paradox of powerlessness? The litany which follows begs answer to the question.

LITURGICAL RESPONSE

"God does not stay angry forever but delights to show mercy" (Micah 7:18b).

The Mass begins. Kyrie eleison. Lord have mercy.

A common theme, a common cry, for common people.

Kyrie eleison. Lord have mercy.

In the prayer of the psalmist in temple and alone.

In the plea of the prophet in promise and persecution.

In the cry of the leper by the roadside,

In the uncivil commotion of the blind beggar at Jericho gate,

In the hand-grasp of silenced voice of a woman bleeding.

Kyrie eleison. Lord have mercy.

In the guilt of those who have broken justice and fractured love by the misuse of their power,

In the shame of those who have been broken by injustice, who have had love withheld

and their creatureliness abused by power's misuse,

The voice, the cry, the claim:

Kyrie eleison. Lord have mercy.

Over centuries, the "Jesus prayer," in Greek, Syriac, Bulgar, Slav, and Russian:

Kyrie eleison. Lord have mercy.

For guilt, we do not self atone.

For shame, we do not self overcome.

One can be forgiven and set free. Mercy can be theirs.

The other can be loved again into worthiness. Mercy can be theirs.

Kyrie eleison. Lord have mercy.

And let us ever remember past and acknowledge present, lest in time, by blindness, deafness, dumbness, and unfeeling to what is, we fail to amend and lose heart even enough to cry out: Kyrie eleison. Lord, have mercy.

CHARGE AND BENEDICTION

Go forth into the world in shalom;
Be of good courage;
Hold fast to what is good and growing;
Do not return abuse for abuse, or evil for evil,
Strengthen the faint hearted;
Support the weak;
Help the afflicted;
Guard the dignity of all people.
Love and serve God with justice,
Rejoicing in the power of the Holy Spirit.
And the blessing of God, the powerful,
Be upon you and remain with you forever.[48]

NOTES

1. See Paul S. Minear, *Images of the Church in the New Testament* (Philadelphia: Westminster Press, 1960).

2. It is not the purpose of this essay to argue the case either way. Rather, focus here is on the ecclesiastical homophobia which so abets violence and abuse towards homosexuals. I would agree with Tony Campolo of Evangelicals for Social Action who has written "Silence is death . . . I believe that those who do not speak up for the gay and lesbian community at this crucial time in history may be lending support to oppression." (*Prism*, 1 (February, 1994), 20).

3. And to be sure, this is not an exclusive categorization. Many other sorts and conditions of persons have experienced hurt at the misuse of ecclesial power. I simply write out of stories recently told to me in my roles as a professor of ministry, director of field education, and spiritual director.

4. Jacquelyn Grant's *White Women's Christ and Black Women's Jesus* (Atlanta: Scholars Press, 1989) has been particularly helpful to me in this regard.

5. *The Complete Poems of Emily Dickinson*, ed. Thomas H. Johnson (Boston: Little, Brown and Company, 1960), 335.

6. *Basic Concepts in Sociology*, ed. H. P. Secher (Secaucus, NJ: The Citadel Press, 1962), 117.

7. May, *Power and Innocence* (New York: W. W. Norton, 1972) and Galbraith, *The Anatomy of Power* (Boston: Houghton Mifflin, 1983).

8. Antonius H. J. Gunneweg and Walter Schmithals, *Authority* (Nashville: Abingdon, 1982), 17 and cf. Bengt Holmberg, "Power and Authority," *Paul and Power* (Philadelphia: Fortress Press, 1978), 125-135.

9. For the following discussion cf. May, 105-113 and Joan Chittister, *Job's Daughters: Women and Power* (New York: Paulist Press, 1990), 11-51.

10. Chittister, 26.

11. Ibid.

12. Ibid., 38.

13. Ibid., 43-44.

14. *Race Matters* (Boston: Beacon Press, 1993), 38.

15. Ibid.

16. May, 112.

17. Lebacqz, *Professional Ethics - Power and Paradox* (Nashville: Abingdon, 1985), 128.

18. Lebacqz, 111, 121. Cf. also Marie M. Fortune, *Is Nothing Sacred? When Sex Invades the Pastoral Relationship* (San Francisco: Harper and Row, 1989) and Marilyn R. Peterson, *At Personal Risk: Boundary Violations in Professional-Client Relationships* (New York: W. W. Norton, 1992).

19. William Ryan, *Blaming the Victim* (New York: Random House, 1976).

20. Quoted in *Fortune*, 122.

21. West, 2.

22. Quoted in Letha Scanzoni and Virginia Mollenkott, *Is the Homosexual My Neighbor?* rev. ed. (San Francisco: Harper, 1994), 6-7.

23. Janet Lundblad, "Towards a Biblical Understanding of Power," *Daughters of Sarah*, 4 (Jan.-Feb., 1978), 2.

24. Ibid.

25. "Bad News, Good News," *The Christian Ministry*, 25 (Sept.-Oct., 1994), 17ff.

26. *The Transfiguration of Politics: The Presence and Power of Jesus of Nazareth In And Over Human Affairs* (New York: Harper and Row, 1975), 69.

27. *In the Name of Jesus* (New York: Crossroad, 1993), 59-60.

28. Martin Hengel, *Christ and Power* (Philadelphia: Fortress Press, 1977), 81.

29. For full treatment of this example, see David W. Augsburger, *Anger and Assertiveness in Pastoral Care* (Philadelphia: Fortress Press, 1979).

30. Paul Tillich, *Love, Power and Justice* (New York: Oxford University Press, 1954).

31. Tillich, 122.

32. I am indebted to my primary mentor in graduate school, Robert C. Worley, for this insight.

33. West, 105.

34. West, 5.

35. May, 118.

36. Alfaro, *Justice and Loyalty* (Grand Rapids: Eerdmans Publishing Co., 1989), 67-68.

37. Ibid.

38. Hans Walter Wolff, *Micah the Prophet* (Philadelphia: Fortress Press, 1981), 109-112. See also Wolff's, *Micah: A Commentary* (Minneapolis: Augsburg, 1990), 179-184.

39. Wolff, *Micah the Prophet*, 112-13.

40. Walter Brueggemann et al., *To Act Justly, Love Tenderly, Walk Humbly: An Agenda For Ministers* (Mahwah, NJ: Paulist Press, 1986), 14-15.

41. Cf. n. 14 above.

42. Walter Brueggemann, *In Man We Trust: The Neglected Side of Biblical Faith* (Atlanta: John Knox Press, 1972), 102.

43. Augsburger, 44-45.

44. West, 63-64.

45. This is a major theme in Cornel West's *Race Matters*. The particular emphases of culture are identified by Marcus J. Borg in his *Meeting Jesus Again For the First Time* (San Francisco: Harper, 1994), 87.

46. Nouwen, 60.

47. For a recent effort in this regard, see Robert C. Bondi, "Crucifixion," *Weavings*, 9 (Sept.-Oct., 1994), 6-27, especially 26-27.

48. Adaptation of a benediction originally written by Robert N. Rodenmayer, *The Pastor's Prayerbook* (New York: Oxford University Press, 1960).

THE PRACTICE OF COMPASSION AND THE DISCIPLESHIP OF EQUALS

ANN O'HARA GRAFF

I would like to explore two metaphors that might benefit our practice of being church. These are the symbol of compassion presented in the phenomenology of Wendy Farley in her recent exploration of theodicy and the discipleship of equals, developed over the past decade by feminist scripture scholar Elisabeth Schüssler Fiorenza.[1] Any assignment to reexamine the identity and mission of the church in the light of scripture and its centuries of interpreters must immediately grapple with the many metaphors that are offered to describe and prescribe what it is to be church. No doubt many of these familiar symbols will be rehearsed in other papers and need not be noted here. However, I will underscore that I find value in the competing metaphors that call for our attention and in the conversation among them. My own selections for this essay represent an interest in the disclosures of two particular symbols, for reasons I will note, and not a dismissal of other possible avenues.

I think it can be simply and directly said that the church is a response to the person and event of Jesus the Christ, and our mission is to witness to the ongoing presence of that event in history. Moreover, central to the event of Jesus the Christ is the revelation that God is love, intimate, indeed incarnate, among us, and at the same time, the transcendent reality that enfolds and exceeds the very cosmos. We are creatures of that love, made able to respond to God in communion with one another. It is in company with these particular and crucial insights that I have chosen to explore the communal response to Jesus the Christ that is the church as the discipleship of equals whose vocation or mission it is to live the compassion of God.

COMPASSION: NAMING THE LOVE OF GOD

While the movement from identity to mission appears to be the logical flow, I would like to begin this study with the symbol of compassion because Farley's phenomenology provides, I find, a helpful avenue into the meaning of the love of God. If this is the love in which we live and to which we witness, then that love indicates both what we are about and who we are with one another.

Farley scrutinizes compassion in the context of theodicy (not ecclesiology). She explores the fact that evil and suffering rend our world in ways unimaginable to many of us, yet that finally incise each and all. She underscores that radical suffering can erode and vitiate our very humanity. In a world in which loss can be profound, though the cry for justice nevertheless rings out, Farley introduces compassion as a power, an efficacy that resists radical suffering and the personal and social evil that corrupts and corrodes.[2] Thus compassion from the outset is more than simply emotion for Farley. It begins there, in sympathy, in the ability to feel with another, to know something of the experience and pain of another, even though we can never fully know another person. Compassion entails feeling and understanding that reaches out of self and toward another. As such, it is a capacity for self-transcendence. Yet, it is more. Compassion is not merely evoked in isolated instances, but, for Farley, is an "enduring disposition." By this she means "a way of organizing and interpreting the world that precedes any particular perception or action."[3] As relational beings who interpret and respond to one another and the world around us, compassion can inform, that is, fundamentally qualify, our consciousness. As such it is a form of love.

Farley suggests that there are three facets of this disposition of love. First, this is love that takes delight in the beloved. It is enjoyment, indeed enchantment with the loveliness of the other. It is also care for the other that arises from what Farley terms a "robust desire" for the other's good and draws courage from that care to act on behalf of the beloved.[4] She then says that this love tends to universality because as an enduring disposition compassion creates a fundamental openness to recognize and care for each and all those whose beauty and pain may be experienced. In a world of conflict such compassion embraces both gazelle and tiger, prey and predator alike. Moreover, its sympathy is not sentiment; it can hold the sinner in love, but clearly condemn destructive acts.

As compassion moves from sympathy to active love as delight and care, Farley engages the language of power. Compassion is efficacious. It is not a power of domination or coercion. Its efficacy is in its ability to resist the ravages of suffering and to effect transformation where possible. Farley explores this particularly in the human sphere.[5] The first gift of compassion is its ability to support the dignity of the sufferer. For a person whose body is being decimated by cancer, for example, this is an essential gift. Yet, as love, compassion must be received and risks rejection. It offers others the empowering power of support for their own primordial integrity and person, but it can be refused.

Rooted in this offer of care and support, compassion becomes an energy to resist suffering and evil and a labor to change suffering to well-being, evil to good. Thus compassion empowers the work of justice to create practical social support for human dignity. Because of the depth of compassion it may make people foolhardy enough to seek the good even when "the powers of hell" are visibly allied against it.

Such, I trust, is a fair outline of Farley's initial phenomenology of compassion. She goes on to redescribe divine love from this starting point.[6] She colors and intensifies it. She chooses the language of ungrounded divine eros, a love that creates the beloved other out of nothingness, and invites her/him into relationship. God risks both creation and relation in the energy of life-giving erotic love. This is not a statement about divine emotion so much as it is about the very nature and perfection of love.[7] In a world characterized by the tragedy of evil and suffering, due in no small part to the inevitable conflicts brought about by finitude and freedom, that love takes on the character of redemptive compassion. While I cannot examine Farley's larger work here, it is necessary to note that the entire first half of her book details her proposals that both creation and freedom are tragically structured. Thus the inherent limits of both the creation itself and human freedom occasion suffering. We experience God, then, both as creator and in compassion, as redeemer of this good and tragic world. This love becomes the redemptive power that resists and transforms the agonies which follow from its own creative act.[8] Compassion is thus a mode of divine relationship as well as an efficacy. Divine compassion is offered continuously to us all. It meets tragic and irreversible loss with the offer of power to resist destruction of one's dignity and the experience of love present even in hellish circumstance. It meets evil, not with simple pardon or failure to judge sin clearly, but with mercy which names the sin, but embraces the sinner and nevertheless offers new life. God's eros is to create, to bind up, to give sight, to heal, to set free, to transform—and it never ends.

If this characterization of divine love is a fair, rough sketch of the primordial cosmic reality which creates us and into which we are drawn—and out of which we do and must live, then this love may indicate our vocation as Christians. Farley points toward this in her use of the language of enduring disposition. Such a disposition describes a way of life, a conformation, or better a school for our being and practice as individuals and as church. In the language of Thomas Aquinas, she describes a habit. What her project does not pursue, but clearly suggests, is that this compassion may be a very good way to describe the habitual way Christians might live, and, since we do not live our faith as individuals alone, but rather are nurtured in it and live it in community, this practice of Christian life may well name the mission of the church. To recap briefly, this would mean that it is the church's mission to incarnate the divine love in the world because we are rooted in and embraced by that love. Thus in every situation we are called to respond with sympathy, with care, and with joy in the other's well-being. We are called to support dignity and integrity and to resist and transform suffering where possible. We are called to name evil resolutely, yet to offer mercy and healing rather than mere retribution. In all cases we are called to support the appropriate rhythms of life.

This form of the work of love appears to conform to the work of Jesus. While Farley does not attempt to link her proposals directly with the narratives of the gospels, connections are readily made. The immediate attention which Jesus gives to those who meet him in need is remarkable throughout the texts. His mission is not abstract; it is concrete. He cared immediately and directly for those who were hungry, sick, disturbed, or endangered. The stories recount that he healed with the gift of restored dignity and inclusion in the community, as well as with physical or mental wholeness. As an example, he healed the bent woman and reminded the leader of the synagoque that she too is a "daughter of Abraham" (Luke 13:10-17). He restored those he touched to family—Jarius's daughter, Peter's mother-in-law, and the widow's son. The entire focus of his encounter with Zacchaeus is Zacchaeus' reconciliation with his fellow townspeople. Apparently, Jesus' sympathy and responsiveness to suffering were keen. The actions the gospels recount appear in the pattern Farley outlines in her discussion of compassion. Jesus' habitual practice of offering the present and tangible love of God appears to be just such a form of enduring, life-giving care for those he met. This love has an absolute priority over every other possible response—such is the gospel's claim, whether in the sophisticated poetry of John or in the tantalizing vingette of the Syro-Phoenician woman who underscored this vocation even for Jesus himself.

For Farley, compassion is the divine response to suffering and the divine disposition in response to evil. Since we are called into this divine practice because we choose to follow Jesus the Christ and to live in his Spirit, my suggestion to characterize the mission of the church as the disposition and practice of compassion may be appropriate to our historical circumstances. Born into the distress of the Roman occupation and journeying into the centuries of Western and even global history, there has been no time that the church has not encountered, endured, and at worst, occasioned, suffering. In our own time, the frenetic pace of living driven by the capitalist greed for profit without regard for persons, community, or the environment is wreaking havoc, both intimate and far-reaching, in this country and elsewhere. The call to compassion requires first a patience, an ability to slow down enough to see and act. Yet in addition to the sheer *agon* of the pace of middle class life in the United States, the hemorrhage of suffering and evil is daily present in its multiple forms of violation, whether in the poverty, drugs and gangs of our cities, or in the toxic substances wasting our environment, or in the continuous and banal but bloody military responses to difficulties in every nation. Our society too often thinks first of jails, police, and retribution and not of healing, help, and alternatives in politics, economics, education, etc. Therefore, compassion must also entail the discernment not only to be vulnerable to the sheer onslaught of suffering detailed relentlessly in the media and met daily in our families and workplaces, but also must be able to choose particular ways of living and acting within the bounds of finitude that might sustain both its disposition and practice. At this juncture reflection on being church through the bonded metaphor of the discipleship of equals may be useful as an explanation of how to live compassion.

COMPASSION AND DISCIPLESHIP

Recently, Elisabeth Schüssler Fiorenza has offered the church the image of the discipleship of equals as a way to understand the nature of relationships that formed the early Christian churches and could inform churches today.[9] In Schüssler Fiorenza's work, the emphasis has been political and ethical: the vocation of every Christian is discipleship, and all disciples, "Jew or Greek, slave or free, male or female" (to paraphrase Gal 3:28) are equal in relation to one another. This is part of the expression of the radical gospel of Jesus.[10] However, before I turn to the political, sexual, and intercultural possibilities this metaphor offers, I would like to pause simply on the notion of discipleship.

Well-worn in the Catholic tradition of spirituality is the image of Mary and Martha, the contemplative sitting at the Master's feet and the active person caring for the needs of the household (Luke 10:38-42). While this imagery has been less than helpful as a story about women's roles and Schüssler Fiorenza's interpretation that this story functioned in Luke's community to protect the teaching role of women as well as their role at the eucharistic table is a vital retrieval,[11] nevertheless there is value in the medieval symbolic usage of the story. The Catholic monastic and mystical traditions, as well as the Pietist and related traditions within Protestantism, lived out of an insight that in our time is being rediscoved in the streams of liberation theology that recognize the necessity of uniting the mystical and the political.

If the mission of the church is to be a praxis of compassion, then we must reflect carefully on the fact that such praxis is always in danger of being disfigured as a duty, a heavy burden, which is easily resented. The fuel of compassion is the experience of being loved compassionately by God, by other people, and through learning love, by oneself. The primary channels for this are both the quality of relations in our intimate lives with family, friends, church community, etc. and contemplative time attentively, wordlessly, open to God in the present moment. The present is the very locus of our enduring relation to God. The first reality of discipleship is attention to the presence of God mediated and incarnated repeatedly in the now. Mary exemplifies this. The second characteristic of discipleship is eucharistic, feeding the household including oneself and the community. Part of feeding the community is to do the work of love for the neighbor. Here is Martha. Love moves in deepening and spreading circles, embracing both the contemplative and active moments. The action of love flows from contemplative experience, but the contemplative, the mystical, is fed by the active, the political. Without this spiral, contemplation can dry up into selfishness, and action can lead to burn out and resentment. The Christian insight is that love is primordial and that love feeds love. Outside of that we are lost.

I would like to pause to note how close this Christian insight is to our Buddhist partners in the human journey. Buddhism is marked by its insistence that wisdom and compassion are joined together. Compassion arises in and is the natural outflow of the seeking of wisdom in right mindfulness and contemplation. Compassion is fed by understanding, and understanding is nourished in mindfulness and meditation which function to help one see what is. The enlightened one, in whom compassion arises, chooses to care continually for others out of love so that they too might experience the joy of understanding. This entails the recognition of the fundamental interrelatedness of all that is, so that one might enter into the work of healing and care. In Buddhism, practice is the key. It is practice of a compassionate way of life that entails mindfulness of the preciousness of the present moment, whether in sitting meditation or in action. I raise this because the insights affirm some of Farley's suggestions and open up an important connection between understanding born in contemplation and compassion.

Thus I am claiming that discipleship has both contemplative and active dimensions, and that specifically, contemplation feeds the experience of love and understanding which create the initial sympathy and compassion. Moreover, the contemplative moment provides patience, perspective, initial discernment, and some rooted strength toward sustained effort to meet suffering and evil with the power of love. While this characterizes personal spiritual experience, it is shaped, sustained, and shared in community. This is clearly the case when one looks at the long tradition of Benedictine life and its many offshoots, at the Buddhist *sangha*, or at the experience of congregations informed by the Devotio Moderna, Pietism, Quakerism, or Methodism. Other models exist in the small faith communities movements in Protestant and Catholic circles, prominent among which are the Latin American *communidades ecclesiales del base*. It is not only possible, but necessary for individuals, that groups of people share forms of common contemplative life. In the Christian tradition this life is constantly nourished and interpreted by word and sacrament and moves outward into encounter with the neighbor.

The second moment of discipleship that I wish to explore is that of action, indeed, interaction with others, and here Schüssler Fiorenza's notion of discipleship of equals becomes a helpful lens. The politics of radical equality demand review. For Fiorenza the praxis of Jesus and the earliest Christians was one that acknowledged all others as persons of equal value, regardless of sex, ethnic group, or position in society. We see the inclusion of women and men in the group of disciples who followed Jesus, and we know women provided for Jesus out of their own resources (Luke 8: 2-3). Fiorenza names and explores the work of many early Christian women like Lydia, Prisca, Chloe, and others who headed household churches and were early evangelists.[12] Her extended arguments indicate that women shared equal value in the earliest churches along with men.

The struggles over inclusion of Jews and Greeks/Gentiles is well documented, and the outcome is clear. The early church again chose equal value, not a hierarchical or exclusive order. Moreover, Dominic Crossan's recent massive scholarly exploration of the social situation in which Jesus preached has led him to emphasize that the historical Jesus proclaimed radical egalitarianism and a "brokerless kingdom of God" in a cultural milieu in which everything required a broker.[13] Everyone is equal, and no one needs to broker their relation to God through anyone else, and for Jesus, argues Crossan, that meant not even through him. Taken together, radical egalitarianism and the brokerless kingdom in which everyone eats at the same table open up an entirely new social world, surely different from the hierarchies of the first century, but also beyond even democratic notions of our own. This, warns Crossan, is not about votes, it is about value.[14] Everyone is absolutely valuable, all the same, and everyone has immediate and equal access to God. Fiorenza and Crossan both dramatically expose the meaning of equal discipleship as a challenge to human social and ecclesial worlds, both in the past and the present.

While it is beyond the purview of this essay to comment on the diverse reconstructions of the historical Jesus, of which Crossan's remains only one, I introduce his work here because it illustrates how precisely this counter-cultural, poor man who lived a compassionate resistance to the bondage of class or person made such an impact that he became the person whom the early Christian community proclaims in its very practice. What the work of Fiorenza and others shows is that they did what he did, and they did it because for him it was the practice of a new world, a new society, God's kingdom. The early Christians, as ourselves, encountered that kingdom through him. Bultmann's famous dictum is correct, "The proclaimer became the proclaimed." This is the trajectory I indicate in pairing Crossan and Fiorenza. The Jesus who so valued people that he would not hold court in his own behalf, instead taught us to be healed healers, to gather in the poor, the blind, and the lame, to be with and for each other. This his followers did, and we do in turn because in him they and we find not only vision and practice, but in and through these, grace. Here is divine love manifest. To proclaim Jesus the Christ of our faith is to do what he did and to recognize God in him and in the deliberate practice of the absolute, non-negotiable value of every single person.

Like the claim that we are all made in the image and likeness of God (Gen 1:26), the practice of a discipleship of equals provides a foundation for our action in relation to each other. Thus if our ecclesial mission is to meet others in whatever situation with compassionate love, the recognition of the radically equal value of every individual so shapes compassion that its sympathy and care cannot be patronizing. Compassion would be disfigured by patriarchal relations, by racism, by class hierarchies based on family or wealth, by homophobia, ageism or by cultural snobbery or efforts to dominate, demean, or dismiss another culture on the basis of some notion of the higher values present in one's own. On the contrary, the discipleship of equals offers both an immediate defining value and a utopian future against which to assess the real situations in which we and others find ourselves. It sets an agenda for the work of compassion that encompasses justice.

Church discipleship as a praxis of attention, compassion, and equality can push us to ask questions about the quality of our relationships with one another: men and women, clerical professionals—especially ministers—and non-professional but committed Christians, church administrators and church people. That kind of examination of relations can also touch even more tender spots which are becoming extremely important in our pluralistic society and in our churches whose membership is drawn from multiple ethnic and racial groups. We must ask what the quality of our relationships is among groups of people with different educational levels, different incomes and different cultural values. We might well ask whether groups with certain educational, economic, or social advantages resist the temptation to presume the greater value of their own position and the concommitant possibility that they will treat others with disdain or contempt or decide to "take care of them" in a way that is finally paternalistic and patronizing.

By contrast, mutual interactions of people conditioned by compassion offer two other kinds of possibilities. One is, following Farley, that we might all learn to take delight in one another, enjoy each other's gifts, and learn from each other's insights born in diverse social and cultural locations. I do not suggest this lightly. Rather, because of my second concern, I know this enjoyment to be costly grace and not cheap gifts easily given and received.

A second concern is to recognize that our mutual relations are far from equal in value whether within this culture, in other cultures, or across cultures. On the contrary our histories, as well as our present, are deeply marred by divisions, domination, long practices of sinful destruction of one another, and the abolition of hope for growth and change. Even the briefest reflection on the patterns of treatment of Native Americans or black people in this culture by whites indicates that the pain among us is profound. Compassion demands that we acknowledge when we have sinned and that we open ourselves to the pain of authentic conversation. Compassion requires work to change socially institutionalized relations, including political, legal, and economic structures that have held people in particular places. Compassion both accepts and names clearly what is and hopes in action for a renewed future.

Such hope must be grounded in the ability to practice mercy as Farley describes it; that is, the ability unflichingly to acknowledge evil, but nonetheless to embrace sinners and be embraced as sinners ourselves. The practice of psychotherapy continues to reveal that healing occurs only when people who have been violated are able to talk about their experience, grieve over it, and give vent to their anger in safe ways. The mission of the church as the practice of compassion both inside and beyond the church walls may be to learn together to hold people's suffering and to seek understanding, hope, and new life. Sin and suffering abound, but here also is the hope of grace abounding. Thus love, work, conversation, mercy, and hope may move us toward social arrangements that secure the equal value of all people. The church as a social institution may incarnate these practices as a discipleship of equals at the same time it labors for social change.

Johannes Baptist Metz has suggested that the church might best be understood as the community in which we are called together to become subjects of a new human history before God.[15] The praxis of compassion suggests a way toward this in our own culture and in our relations with other cultures. In the latter situation, not only do the wounds of colonialism and exploitation cry for healing, but also the practices of missionaries which did harm, whether ideologues who extended the work of the *conquistador* and other military conquerors, or those who were unable to distinguish between Christianity and western culture and demanded that native identity be relinquished when people accepted the new religion. Insofar as the praxis of compassion is a practice of the gospel of Jesus in action, we westerners are only beginning to recognize that valuing others equally means we are not and should not try to be in control of the fertile event of the Word of God as it takes root in other cultures. Again, the path to authentic conversation is through the morass of sin and suffering, as well as in the delights of difference and the discovery of friends.

In all this, I suggest that an ecclesial identity as a discipleship of equals, one which emphasizes both its mystical and political dimensions and equality, raises both a vision of renewed human relations and an ethical agenda. The metaphors inform and are informed by the church's mission to practice compassion as a mode of living the gospel. It is in compassion that we witness to and incarnate the work of Jesus. In compassion we live in and offer the gifts of divine love.

NOTES

1. See Farley, *Tragic Vision and Divine Compassion: A Contemporary Theodicy* (Louisville: Westminster/John Knox Press, 1990); see also Fiorenza, *In Memory of Her: A Feminist Reconstruction of Christian Origins* (New York: Crossroad, 1983), and *Discipleship of Equals: Critical Feminist Ekklesia-logy of Liberation* (New York: Crossroad, 1993).

2. In the first few sentences I have pointed toward the first half of Farley's book, entitled, *Tragedy, Suffering and the Problem of Evil.* In the description of compassion that follows I walk through her chapter, "A Phenomenology of Compassion," pp. 69-94.

3. Farley, 73.

4. Ibid., 77.

5. I think her position could readily be extended to include ecological concerns, but she does not press these.

6. Farley, 95-133.

7. Although Farley does not note this, her position is close to the ancient theologies of the Neo-Platonic tradition exemplified by that of the Pseudo-Dionysius, so influential in the West, which claim that God/the Good essentially gives itself to all that is. This insight into divine goodness/love as essentially self-communicating is repeated in Bonaventure, Thomas, and most recently and powerfully in Karl Rahner (See his *Foundations of Christian Faith,* trans. by William V. Dych (New York: The Seabury Press, 1978.)

8. Farley, 107.

9. See both *In Memory of Her* and *Discipleship of Equals.*

10. *In Memory,* 205-241.

11. Ibid., 165-166.

12. See *In Memory of Her,* Parts II and III.

13. John Dominic Crossan, *The Historical Jesus: The Life of a Mediterranean Jewish Peasant* (San Francisco: Harper 1991), 225-426. See also *Jesus: A Revolutionary Biography* San Francisco: Harper 1994). The reader should be clear, as Crossan is throughout, that his is an historical reconstruction, not a christology. Christians have to wrestle with both alternative reconstructions of the historical Jesus and multiple constructions of the Christ of faith. What we say of Jesus Christ belongs to that dialectic. See *Jesus,* 199-200.

14. He made this point explicity in a public conference, "Jesus and Faith," at DePaul University, Feb. 4-5, 1993.

15. *Faith in History and Society: Toward a Practical Fundamental Theology* (New York: The Seabury Press, 1980), 136-153.

THE CHURCH: BORN TO HELP SEEKERS FIND WHOLENESS

DONALD M. WARDLAW

And they were amazed and wondered, saying....
we hear them telling in our own tongues the
mighty works of God. Acts 2:7, 11.

The birth of the church comes off almost as dramatic counterpoint
to the splendid erudition and deep cognition
about the church these past two days.
For the church was born in wind, fire, and babble.
Frankly, I am more at home with well-reasoned ecclesiologies,
bolstered by endnotes and bibliographies,
than I am with the frenzied swirl of the upper room.
Such a raw scene does not jibe well with literate sensibilities.
Why not just slip quietly out of the upper room, down the stairs,
and on back to the library stacks and research regimen.
Why not let some holy roller go up there in our place
to dance in the wind and go crazy with the fire.

But there is a deeper sense in which we all belong in that room.
For the genetic pool of our spirituality
that has lent such passion to our research and sharing
came into full force and focus that first Pentecost.
We were there when all heaven broke loose.

Do you remember the strange calm before the Spirit came?
We sit in that upper room in expectant silence.
Quite a contrast to the hubbub of a million seekers
down there in the streets, Jews from everywhere,
Phyrgia, Egypt, Cappadocia, Judea, Libya...
A million seekers after God's wholeness and peace.

Here we are above the jostle and hum of seekers,
hunkered down in our quiet space.
Actually, for all our learning, we are rather simple followers.

No super spirits in this room, really.
Simon Peter: ordinary businessman with a few boats.
Matthew: bureaucrat, tax man, on leave from the tax office.
Simon the Zealot: political activist, motivator.
On around, James, John, Andrew, and other disciples,
    and the women, and about 100 others.
Whatever our persona, we are simple, kind of ordinary up here.

So we sit and wait.
We sit with Christ's promise, not sure what the Spirit
    will look or feel like when Pentecost hits.
All we know is Christ promised to empower us for mission
    and so we wait prayerfully, expectantly, silently.

Then the Spirit breaks loose—
God's order exploding into our order,
A deafening, thundering sound like a Kansas tornado.
A rush of warm wind slams us all into a huddle
    making our hair stand on end.

Crackling streaks of flame pop and dance about our heads
    as we clutch at one another in fear and awe.
Finally, the swirl of heat and thunder above our heads
    turns into a pressure cooker within us that explodes
        in acts we never knew we were capable of.
Now we are on our feet, tumbling down the stairs,
    driven by the Spirit out into the melee of seekers
        in the streets below.
Surprising words start tumbling from our mouths.
We have had no chance to polish the syntax or check the footnotes.
We are talking in other people's language,
    standing eye-to-eye with Parthians, Medes,
        Pamphylians, Romans, Cretans, Arabians,
    telling them about the *shalom* that God gives
        putting it all in their own thought frame,
        their own symbol system, their own language.
Driven to help seekers find wholeness. That is Pentecost!

II

Now look again today out the windows of that upper room.
The Parthians, the Medes, the Pamphylians are still down there
    in the streets, hungering for *shalom*, for peace and justice,
        craving for personal and communal wholeness.
Up here in this room you and I wait again for the Spirit.
We are not feeling all that special spiritually
    any more than we were that first Pentecost.

O we are capable all right. Our resumés read well,
with the degrees earned, the books and articles written,
the deep thinking, speeches made, movements sparked.
But still, we are pretty ordinary in things of the Spirit.

In the quiet of this expectation, you and I sit over in the
corner and begin to share with each other
at levels beyond expected scholarly shop talk.
You tell me that, like Peter, James, and John,
you have tried to follow Jesus, but only so much of it
really "takes."
You followed Jesus' call to seminary and grad school.
You have done time for Jesus in recalcitrant churches.
You have cried out for Jesus in hundreds of sermons and seminars.
You have given money to Jesus, gotten into faculty fights
for Jesus, risked your marriage for Jesus.
Still, something is missing.
While he sweat blood at Gethsemane, you confess
that you fell asleep nearby, just as I did.
You confess that you, just as I, stand aside and watch,
while he is crucified again and again at City Hall,
Capitol Hill, or even denominational headquarters,
while he gets nailed over and again in seminary halls,
or even at your own breakfast table.

You confess to me about yourself what is true about myself.
That for all our following, the wholeness is not there.
As God's people we know we do not have our act together.
O we have enjoyed some power and effectiveness
in our teaching, writing, preaching, leadership.
But there is a spiritual fullness that is missing.
Where is the Pentecost that will open the flow of personal,
emotional, and spiritual power within us?
Where is the Pentecost that will so ground us in our souls
that we will be able to transcend our fears and anxieties
and trust this strange band of believers around us?
So we sit in the upper room and wait for Pentecost.

And then, the Spirit breaks loose.
God's order explodes into our order like a tornado rearranging
the landscape of our corporate and private psyche.
Wind and fire sweep through this upper room of our
habitual spirituality to upset the self-protective scene
we have built around ourselves.

Maybe your Pentecost begins with the wind and fire
that sweeps through your soul as a career crisis,
in some cases destroying trust between you and colleagues,
in other cases radically rearranging possibilities
for effective campus or pastoral relationships.
But in the wake of the pain and struggle, you are learning
what it means at deep levels to be faithful.
You are seeing how even through the wind and fire
God's Spirit is moving you toward wholeness.

Or, maybe your Pentecost begins with the wind and fire
that shakes your personal faith to its foundations,
when you are told you have an incurable disease,
or when the well-honed theology turns to ashes in your mouth,
or when the church for which you have have given so much
seems less loving than the Rotary Club nearby.
Maybe your Pentecost begins with wind and fire
that ravages your family life,
when the spouse wants to sue the church for alienation of
affection, or when the kids act as if there is no
place
for Christ in their lives.
But now, after much prayer and the encircling love of others,
you are beginning to see the flames that once seemed to
consume your faith as the very fires that purified your faith.
You are seeing how even through the wind and fire
God's Spirit is moving you toward wholeness.

III

But now comes the climax of this Pentecost.
Now comes the swirl of wind and fire above our heads
that turns into a pressure cooker within us
that explodes into action we as a body of believers
never dreamed we were capable of.
At some point we are on our feet, down the stairs,
reaching out to seekers in the streets below.
And what is amazing is how readily and naturally you and I
find ourselves speaking the language of those seekers.
To share with seekers in their own language the gifts of wholeness.
What a gift of the Holy Spirit to be able to do that!

We are speaking another's language by learning to enter deeply
into that other person's world to promote wholeness.

Remember how as professor or pastor we were once confident
to prescribe to our students or parishioners precisely how they should think about Jesus and the Church, or how they should behave at home or the office.
But then the wind and fire of Pentecost comes and surprisingly
we begin to find ourselves speaking more in their tongues than our own.
We begin to be able to see inside what it means to be a woman
in this society and the many ways that abuse happens.
We begin to be able to see inside what it means to be of color
in this society and the many ways discrimination happens.
We begin to be able to see inside what it means to be poor
in this society and the many ways economic oppression happens.
O, for all our cleverness as students, scholars, teachers,
the irony is we never sat down and figured out
how to speak the language of the seekers.
No, wind and fire came thundering through us and among us
and *gave us* the tongues to enter into the seeker's world.
No, wind and fire came roaring through our little fellowship
and in spite of all our bickering and power plays
turned us into a community of possibility
for living the alternative world of the gospel.
So, do you wonder if there is a place for you in the upper room
at Pentecost.
You and I know we have a place up there in that room
when we come to know ourselves as seekers.
Better still, when we begin to feel the wind of the Spirit
against our face and the fire of the Spirit in our souls.
That is when we begin to find ourselves as seekers
speaking the language of other seekers,
offering the gift of wholeness.
That is when the church is born, again, and again, and again.

LITANY

Leader: O God, we tremble when we think of the church. We tremble at both the privilege of being the community of God and at our failure to live up to our calling.

People: Forgive us for using such language as "people of God" or "chosen" either arrogantly or glibly.

Leader: God, your desire to have a people amazes us. The love motivating you surprises us.

People: Teach us once again who we are in your purposes.

Leader: Help us to know in new ways on whom we are founded and from whom we take our identity—the Christ who died and was raised on our behalf.

People: Help us to know that love received from you must be extended to others—that we have a responsibility and a mission.

Leader: That we have good news to share and good news to live and your Spirit to energize us.

People: May our community model your grace, express your caring, and transcend our divisions.

Leader: Do not let us be conformed to life around us. Help us seek justice, show mercy, and live humbly before you. Let your wind and fire move us.

People: Help us to follow our Lord Christ. Keep calling us, keep renewing us, keep shaping us so that our life together is praise and a sweet offering to you. Use us, Lord. Use even us. Amen.

BIBLIOGRAPHY ON THE CHURCH*

Achtemeier, Paul J. *The Quest for Unity in the New Testament Church: A Study in Paul and Acts*. Philadelphia: Fortress Press, 1987. This is a theological and historical examination of the problems the early church faced concerning the nature and extent of its unity. The books of Acts and Galatians receive primary attention.

Avis, Paul D. L. *The Church in the Theology of the Reformers*. Atlanta: John Knox Press, 1981. Avis deals with three aspects of Reformation ecclesiology: the doctrine of "the true church" and its marks; the structure of the ministry of the church; and the rise of the Protestant missionary concern.

Banks, Robert J. *Paul's Idea of Community: The Early House Churches in their Historical Setting*. Grand Rapids: Eerdmans, 1980. Although not a technical investigation, this is a substantive analysis of the meaning and practice of community as it appears in Paul's letters. Banks places Paul within his sociological context and compares him with his contemporaries.

Barrett, C. K. *Church, Ministry, and Sacraments in the New Testament*. Grand Rapids: Eerdmans, 1985. The content of this book was originally four lectures dealing with the unity of the church. In addition to discussing the character of ministry and the role of the sacraments, the author treats the transition from Jesus to the church and the development that takes place within the NT and apostolic fathers.

Barth, Markus. *Israel and the Church: Contribution to a Dialogue Vital for Peace*. Richmond: John Knox Press, 1969. Barth attempts to come to grips with some of the issues in the Jewish-Christian debate. He deals with questions regarding the Messiah, the Bible, the nature of obedient faith, and the basis of community and peace.

Barth, Markus. *The People of God*. Journal for the Study of the New Testament Supplement Series, 5. Sheffield: JSOT Press, 1983. Barth deals with the problems posed by Paul's statements on the people of God, the unity of this people, and the resulting consequences.

Best, Ernest. *One Body in Christ: a Study in the Relationship of the Church to Christ in the Epistles of the Apostle Paul*. London: SPCK, 1955. Best provides a classic treatment of expressions such as "in Christ," "with Christ," "into Christ," "body of Christ," and "bride of Christ" in order to define the relationship between Christ and his Church.

Birkey,Del. *The House Church: A Model for Renewing the Church*. Scottdale: Herald Press, 1988. This is an attempt to balance a vertical theology of revelation with a horizontal theology of relationships. Birkey uses the first house churches as a model for contemporary ministry in the hope of revitalizing today's churches.

Bloesch, Donald G. *Crumbling Foundations*. Grand Rapids: Zondervan, 1984. Bloesch is concerned about the moral and spiritual decay in western culture and seeks to fortify Christians and the witness of the Church.

Boff, Leonardo. *Church, Charism, and Power: Liberation and the Institutional Church*. Translated by John Diercksmeier. New York: Crossroad, 1985. This Latin American liberation analysis and critique of the institutional church caused controversy, but also calls for new models of the church focused on the poor and issues of justice.

---

*Appreciation is expressed to Nathan Pawl for his work in compiling and annotating most of this bibliography.

Boff, Leonardo. *Ecclesiogenesis: The Base Communities Reinvent the Church.* Translated by Robert R. Barr. Maryknoll: Orbis, 1986. Boff reacts against the institutional church and emphasizes the role of the laity in carrying forward the mission of the church. He argues for a participationist model of the church and also discusses the sacraments and the role of women in the church.

Brooks, Stephenson H. *Matthew's Community.* Journal for the Study of the New Testament Supplement Series. Sheffield: JSOT Press, 1987. This is a technical study of select Matthean sayings in an attempt to reconstruct the Matthean community.

Brown, Raymond E. *The Churches the Apostles Left Behind.* New York: Paulist Press, 1984. Brown investigates the early Christian communities from the viewpoint of their diverse understanding of what was important for survival and growth after the death of the apostles. He treats such topics as church structure, the body of Christ, and the people of God.

Carson, D. A. *The Church in the Bible and the World: An International Study.* Grand Rapids: Baker Book House, 1987. This is a collection of essays by evangelical scholars on topics related to the identity and mission of the church. Most of the articles are biblically oriented discussions of the church, its worship, and its ministry.

Cerfaux, L. *The Church in the Theology of St. Paul.* Translated by Geoffrey Webb and Adrian Walker. Freiburg: Herder and Herder, 1959. This is a major attempt to write a Pauline theology of the church. Cerfaux divides his treatment into three sections: God's people; Christian experience; and the church heavenly. The last section discusses the element of mystery in the theology of the church.

Clements, R. E. *God's Chosen People: A Theological Interpretation of the Book of Deuteronomy.* London: SCM, 1968. This book discusses Israel's special relationship with God and treats such issues as the covenant of God with his people, divine election, worship, and such gifts of God as the land, the law, and the prophets.

Cole, Alan. *The Body of Christ: A New Testament Image of the Church.* Philadelphia: Westminster Press, 1964. Cole gives a brief biblical study which examines the significance of the metaphorical description of the church as the body of Christ.

Davies, Horton, ed. *Studies of the Church in History: Essays Honoring Robert S. Paul on his Sixty-fifth Birthday.* Allison Park, PA: Pickwick Publications, 1983. These articles deal with a variety of topics that intersect with ecclesiology: biblical subjects; the Cappodocians; English preaching; aspects of church life in Canada, America, and Australia; ecumenicity; and specific articles on P. T. Forsyth and on Horace Bushnell's congregation.

Dieter, Melvin E. and Berg, Daniel N., eds. *The Church: An Inquiry into Ecclesiology from a Biblical-Theological Perspective.* Vol.4: Wesleyan Theological Perspectives. Anderson: Warner Press, 1972. This collection of essays seeks to provide a biblical, theological, historical, and practical understanding of the church. Three of the articles deal with the ecclesiology of John Wesley.

Doohan, Helen. *Paul's Vision of Church.* Wilmington: Michael Glazier, 1989. This book examines the growth of the early church, the church's character in the first century, Paul's experience in specific communities, and the essential components in his ecclesiology.

Downing, Gerald F. *The Church and Jesus: A Study in History, Philosophy, and Theology. Studies in Bib--lical Theology,* Second Series. London: SCM Press, 1968. Downing's book focuses on the quest for the historical primitive church. He deals with the methodological issues in such a quest more than with a resultant ecclesiology.

Dudley, Carl S. and Hilgert, Earle. *New Testament Tensions and the Contemporary Church.* Philadelphia: Fortress Press, 1987. The authors focus on the tensions in the NT church in order to deal with issues that face contemporary congregations: community formation, counterculture Christianity, faith crisis and witnessing, using conflict constructively, and the use of rituals.

Dulles, Avery Robert. *Models of the Church.* Revised edition. Garden City, NY: Doubleday, 1987. Writing from a Roman Catholic perspective, Dulles gives a comparative ecclesiology using a number of different models in order to deal with such topics as mystical communion, sacraments, eschatology, and revelation. This revised edition includes a chapter on the church as a community of disciples.

Dulles, Avery. *The Resilient Church: The Necessity and Limits of Adaptation.* Garden City, NY, 1977. In this work Dulles assesses Catholic ecclesiology since Vatican II and seeks to move it forward. He discusses nine issues, but the underlying theme is the mission of the church to be nothing other than the church.

Esler, Philip Francis. *Community and Gospel in Luke-Acts: The Social and Political Motivations of Lucan Theology.* Cambridge: Cambridge University Press, 1987. This book deals with the social and political influences on Luke's theology and the identity of his community. It also explores the use of "law," the temple, Luke's theology of the poor and rich, and the view of ancestral politics in Rome.

Flew, R. Newton. *Jesus and His Church: A Study of the Idea of the Ecclesia in the New Testament.* New York: Abingdon Press, 1938. This is a classic treatment of the church in the New Testament in which Flew attempts to discern the central idea of the ecclesia. He deals with the question of whether there is room for the idea of ecclesia in the teaching of Jesus, with the history of the early church and with the teaching of the apostles.

Forsyth, P. T. *The Church and the Sacraments.* London: Independent Press, 1955. This is a collection of lectures on Forsyth's views of the church and the sacraments. Forsyth writes from a Free Church tradition and deals with issues such as unity, baptism, and communion.

Gager, J. G. *Kingdom and Community: The Social World of Early Christianity.* Englewood Cliffs, N.J.: Prentice-Hall, 1975. This book is rooted in the conception of early Christianity as a social world in the making. It explores such topics as the relationship between religion and social status, the enthusiastic character of the earliest Christian communities, transformation into religious and social institutions, and the emergence of Christianity as the dominant religion of the Roman Empire.

Hall, Douglas John. *The Future of the Church: Where are We Headed ?* The United Church Publishing House, 1989. This study examines the history of the church in order to lay a foundation for the church's future. It describes responses to the discouragement Christians have been conditioned to assume and the potential for the future of the church in being a cruciform body of Christ.

Halton, Thomas. *The Church.* Wilmington: Michael Glazier, 1985. Halton gives a patristic commentary on the Lumen Gentium, the magisterial document devoted to the subject of the church by the Second Vatican Council in 1964. The author presents quotations from the church fathers to explain the mystery of the church.

Hanson, Anthony T. *The Church of the Servant.* London: SCM Press, 1962. This small book is an examination of the idea of servanthood from the perspectives of Israel, Jesus, and the NT church. The intent is to remind the present church of its servant character.

Hanson, Anthony. *The Meaning of Unity: A Study of a Biblical Theme.* London: The Highway Press, 1954. Hanson presents an examination of the idea of unity in both testaments in order to explain the basis of the unity of the church.

Hanson, Paul D. *The People Called: The Growth of Community in the Bible.* San Francisco: Harper & Row, 1987. This is thorough study of both testaments focused on the notion of living together in community. Hanson views this idea as the unifying theme of the Bible. He deals with a wide diversity of theological traditions (i.e., priestly, sapiental, and apocalyptic) and the unique contributions they make in the Bible.

Hanson, Stig. *The Unity of the Church in the New Testament: Colossians and Ephesians*. Uppsala, 1946. This dissertation analyzes the idea of unity in two epistles where the subject is emphasized, but over half the book treats material outside Ephesians and Colossians. Hanson investigates the OT and Judaism, Jesus teaching in the synoptics, and Paul's teaching in other letters. Hanson finds eschatology to be characteristic of the biblical conception of unity.

Harrington, Daniel J. *The Light of All Nations: Essays on the Church in New Testarnent Research.* Wilmington: Michael Glazier, 1982. This is a collection of essays on the church in the NT. It is an attempt to give a record of some of the major issues facing the church in recent years.

Harrington, D. J. *God's People in Christ: New Testament Perspectives on the Church and Judaism.* Philadelphia: Fortress Press, 1980. Harrington explores the biblical foundations for the concept of the church as the people of God and the special relationship that it implies the church has with God. He focuses on specific texts and attempts to find the original meaning and its relevance for today.

Harrison, Everett F. *The Apostolic Church.* Grand Rapids: Eerdmans, 1985. This is a topical study on the developments in the early years of the life of the Christian church. It is divided into sections on gospel history and apostolic history.

Hinson, Glenn E. *Understanding of the Church.* Philadelphia: Fortress Press, 1986. Hinson attempts to give a better understanding of the church and an appreciation of how Christianity of the twentieth century still reflects the first church. He plots the historical basis on which the modern church is based by using material from the church fathers. He deals with topics such as martyrdom, unity, apostolic tradition, prayer, and baptism.

Hodgson, Peter. *Revisioning the Church: Ecclesial Freedom in the New Paradigm.* Philadelphia: Fortress Press, 1988. The author argues that a new paradigm is emerging because of various crises that modern society and the modern church have experienced. He seeks to work out a theology of the church in the context of this new paradigm.

Jay, Eric G. *The Church: Its Changing Image Through Twenty Centuries.* Atlanta: John Knox Press, 1977. By tracing the history of the church Jay attempts to answer the questions about the church's identity and purpose. He provides a historical study of doctrine broken into six periods: the NT church, the patristic period, the medieval period, the Reformation, the eighteenth and nineteenth centuries, and the twentieth century.

Jervell, Jacob. *Luke and the People of God: A New Look at Luke-Acts.* Minneapolis: Augsburg Publishing House, 1972. The central theme of these essays is Luke's ecclesiology, the identity of the church as heir to the promises of Israel, and the alienation of Jewish Christians due to the rumors about Paul.

Käsemann, E. "Ministry and Community in the New Testament," *Essays on New Testament Themes.* Translated by W. J. Montague. Philadelphia: Fortress Press, 1982. This is an important essay showing the basis, character, and activity of the church. The same volume has an essay on the canon and the unity of the church.

Keck, Leander. The *Church Confident: Christianity Can Repent, but It Must not Whimper.* Nashville: Abingdon, 1993. This book was originally lectures addressing the subject of the renewal of mainline Protestantism. After describing the malaise afflicting mainline Protestantism, Keck treats four major subjects and their importance for the modern church: worship; theology; ethos; and communication.

Kolbenschlag, Madonna. *Authority, Community and Conflict.* Kansas City: Sheed and Ward, 1986. This is a collection of documents from the Vatican and the Sisters of Mercy concerning three sisters who pursued political office. It looks at the political, social, and theological impact that surrounded this conflict.

Kress, Robert. *The Church: Communion, Sacrament, Communication.* New York: Paulist Press, 1985. Seeking to avoid previous controversies about the church, the author argues for the origin of the church in the saving will of God. In addition to chapters that focus on the three topics of the title, a chapter is devoted to God and religion.

Kromminga, John H. *All One Body We: The Doctrine of the Church in Ecumenical Perspective*. Grand Rapids: Eerdmans, 1970. This is a look at a divided church and the doctrines that caused the divisions. This book seeks to answer the questions about the church's future and its present existence. It attempts to determine whether anything has happened to the respective ecclesiologies over the past forty years.

Küng, H. *The Church*. New York: Sheed & Ward, 1967. Kung seeks to answer the question how we know the church is on the right path. He seeks to discern what the church of today should be in light of the gospel. He examines the history, eschatology, structure, and offices of the church.

Kung, Hans and Swidler, Leonard. *The Church in Anguish: Has the Vatican Betrayed Vatican II?* San Francisco: Harper & Row, 1986. This is a collection of essays, mainly by Catholic theologians, showing the sharp contrast between the church of today and that of Vatican II.

Lacocque, André. *But as for Me: The Question of Election in the Life of God 's People Today*. Atlanta: John Knox Press, 1973. Lacocque deals with the question what it means to be called by God. His study of the theology of election seeks to recover the true identity of the church. He examines suffering, self sacrifice, and commitment.

Lohfink, Gerhard. *Jesus and Community*. Translated by John P. Galvin. Philadelphia: Fortress Press, 1982. This is an examination of the relationship between Jesus and Israel and of Jesus and his disciples. Lohfink also discusses the role of discipleship in the ancient church.

Macdonald, Margaret, Y. *The Pauline Churches: A Socio-historical Study of Institutionalization in the Pauline and Deutero-Pauline Writings*. Cambridge: Cambridge University Press, 1988. This is a socio-historical study which traces the institutionalization of various aspects of community life.

Martin, Ralph P. *The Family and the Fellowship: New Testament Images of the Church*. Grand Rapids: Eerdmans, 1979. This is a summary of NT images of the church and its role in the believer's life.

Martin, Ralph P. *The Spirit and the Congregation: Studies in I Corinthians 12-15*. Grand Rapids: Eerdmans,1984. Martin attempts to answer the questions how we should deal with charismatic claims that speaking in tongues authenticates one's Christianity and with Paul's writings on women's roles in the church. He also addresses the issue of whether public worship in mainstream denominations is at odds with Pauline thought.

McKelvey, R. J. *The New Temple: The Church in the New Testament*. London: Oxford University Press, 1969. This is a discussion of the church as God's new temple. It provides a thorough examination of the idea of the temple in the OT, the NT, and noncannonical writings.

Meyer, Ben F. *The Church in Three Tenses*. Garden City, NY: Doubleday, 1971. Meyer attempts to answer the question what the Christian is to believe with respect to the church. He addresses the question with reference to the past, present and future.

Minear, Paul S. *Images of the Church in the New Testament*. Philadelphia: Westminster Press, 1960. This classic treatment analyzes 96 images of the church in the NT to develop an ecclesiology. In addition to analyzing the images and their interrelation, Minear provides instruction in understanding and interpreting images.

Moltmann, Jürgen. *The Church in the Power of the Spirit*. Minneapolis: Fortress Press, 1993. Moltmann gives an interpretation of the theological traditions of the church. He intends to confront the insecurities of a church dealing with rapid change in external circumstances, the progress of science and technology, and a simultaneously growing threat through social, military and ecological conflicts.

Nygren, Anders, ed. *This is the Church*. Translated by Carl C. Rasmussen. Philadelphia: Muhlenberg Press, 1952. Nygren discusses three theological issues facing the church: the doctrine of the nature of the church, the nature of the word of God, and the evangelical view of the sacraments.

O'Grady, Colm. *The Church in Catholic Theology: Dialogue with Karl Barth.* London: Geoffrey Chapman,1969. O'Grady uses Karl Barth's doctrine of the church to question and reshape current Catholic ecclesiology. He also critiques Barth's ecclesiology.

Panikulam, G. *Koinonia in the New Testament: A Dynamic Expression of Christian Life.* Rome: Biblical Institute Press, 1979. This is an in-depth study of fellowship in the NT. It discusses such specifics as koinonia with the Son, the body and blood of Christ, the Spirit, scripture, faith, and the collection .

Pannenberg, Wolfhart. *The Church.* Translated by Keith Crim. Philadelphia: Westminster Press, 1983. This is an examination of the unity of the church, the theological and doctrinal issues surrounding it and the decline in church attendance.

Rikhof, Herwi. *The Concept of Church: A Methodological Inquiry into the Use of Metaphors in Ecclesiol--ogy.* London: Sheed and Ward, 1981. This is a study of Lumen Gentium, the dogmatic description of the church. He surveys a number of publications dealing with this document.

Robinson, John A. T. *The Body: A Study in Pauline Theology.* Studies in Biblical Theology. London: SCM Press, 1952. Robinson writes this book for two reasons: 1) to study humanity and the pertinence of the gospel; 2) to treat the Pauline concept of the body in its social, political, and religious implications.

Roetzel, Calvin J. *Judgment in the Community: A Study of the Relationship between Eschatology and Ec clesiology in Paul.* Leiden: Brill, 1972. This book creates an eschatological model to inform and guide the church. It discusses the relationship between judgment and the church and shows how this idea is closely linked to Jewish thought.

Russell, Letty M. *Church in the Round.* Louisville: Westminster/John Knox Press, 1993. Russell describes a community of faith working to embody God's new creation by becoming partners with those who are on the fringe of society and church.

Sampley, J. Paul. *Pauline Partnership in Christ: Christian Community and Commitment in Light of Roman Law.* Philadelphia: Fortress Press, 1980. This is an identification and analysis of Paul's use of partnership as a model of Christian community. It deals with the issues of Christian freedom, imitation of Paul, the collection for the saints, Paul's support for his preaching, and his claims about Timothy and Titus.

Schillebeeckx, Edward. *Church: The Human Story of God.* London: SCM Press, 1990. This book was intended to be an ecclesiological third part of a trilogy Jesus—Christ—Church, but conflict with the Roman Catholic Church led to changes. Much more space is given to the heart of the gospel and the Christian religion, especially to language and revelation, to humanity's search for God, and God's search for humaity, and to the mission of Jesus. The last is offered as the basis of the church, and attention is given to the democratic rule of the church as the community of God.

Schnackenburg, Rudolph. *The Church in the New Testament.* New York: Herder and Herder, 1965. This is a work in four parts which attempts to trace the nature and mystery of the church. It deals with the fundamental characteristics, the theology, the essential features, and the mystery of the church.

Schneider, Johannes. *Church and World in the New Testament.* Macon: Mercer University Press, 1983. Schneider presents a NT perspective on how the church and the world are both opposed and related to each other. He includes treatments of the relation of church and state, of husband and wife, of parent and child, of Christians and possessions, and of personal behavior of the Christian in the world.

Schwarz, Hans. *The Christian Church.* Minneapolis: Augsburg, 1982. In order to prepare for the church's future, the author discusses briefly the origin of the church and the structure of the NT church, but the bulk of this work is a historical, systematic approach to the church's character and mission.

Schweizer, Eduard. *Church Order in the New Testament.* London: SCM Press, 1979. Schweizer presents a comprehensive examination of the church in the NT and the apostolic fathers. He treats both the diversity of views and the unity found in these writings. He also discusses issues relating to church office, ministry, and ordination.

Schweizer, Eduard. *The Church as the Body of Christ.* Richmond: John Knox Press, 1964. This is an attempt to describe what members of the early Christian Church thought when they spoke about the body of Christ. Included is a treatment of the NT understanding of humanity.

Seitz, Oscar J. F. *One Body and One Spirit: A Study of the Church in the New Testament.* Greenwich: Seabury Press, 1960. This is a brief overview of the first church, Jesus and his congregation in Israel, and the growth and development of the church.

Shaw, Joseph M. *The Pilgrim People of God: Recovering a Biblical Motif.* Minneapolis:Augsburg, 1990. Shaw attempts to show that God approaches the human race by creating a people who are to worship and bear witness to him. He traces the theme of the people of God throughout the Bible and the church's history.

Sobrino, Jon. *The True Church and the Poor.* Translated by Matthew J. O'Connell. Maryknoll: Orbis Books, 1984. This is not an ecclesiology, but rather an attempt to shed light from a Latin-American perspective on basic problems faced by the church.

Steinmetz, David G. *Memory and Mission.* Nashville: Abingdon, 1988. In nine essays Steinmetz deals with the problem of collective amnesia in American Protestant Churches. He addresses a church that has a passion for action over thought and whose agendas are often set by secular culture.

Tillapaugh, Frank R. *The Church Unleashed.* Ventura: Regal Books, 1982. Tillapaugh analyzes the unique methods of growth in the Bear Valley Baptist Church in the late 70's and early 80's. He presents the strategy and structures used to bring about renewal and in the process treats a variety of topics, from identifying target groups to developing a global vision.

Tonkin, John. *The Church and the Secular Order in Reformation Thought.* New York: Colombia University Press, 1971. This is a treatment of the Reformers' thoughts concerning the problem of the institutional church. It deals with the theological, eschatological, and christological views of the church as an institution in the writings of Martin Luther, John Calvin, and Menno Simons.

Watson, David. *I Believe in the Church.* Grand Rapids: Eerdmans, 1978. This is not a theological treatise but rather a biblical treatment of what God intends the church to be. The author seeks a renewal of a church that has lost confidence and credibility. He also treats the current differences between Roman Catholics and other communities.

Williams, Colin W. *The Church.* New Directions in Theology Today, Volume IV. Philadelphia: Westminster Press, 1952. Williams looks at the changing role of the church in a changing world. He examines the traditional and dogmatic approaches of various groups (Catholic, classical Protestant, and Free Church) and also treats the structures found in each.

Yorke, Gosnell L. O. R. *The Church as the Body of Christ in the Pauline Corpus: A Reexamination.* Lanham, MD: University Press of America, 1991. Yorke reexamines Paul's use of "body." He investigates the relation of Christ's risen body and the church as body and also the use of "head" in relation to body. He not only provides an overview of the discussion, but also treats the relevant passages in 1 Corinthians, Romans, Ephesians, and Colossians.

NORTH PARK THEOLOGICAL SEMINARY

SYMPOSIUM ON THE THEOLOGICAL INTERPRETATION OF SCRIPTURE

OCTOBER 14-16, 1994

THE CHURCH

THE PRESENTERS

FRANÇOIS BOVON
Harvard Divinity School, Cambridge, MA (New Testament)

CARL BRAATEN
Lutheran School of Theology at Chicago, Chicago, IL (Systematic Theology)

RICHARD CARLSON
North Park Theological Seminary, Chicago, IL (Practical Theology)

RICHARD HAYS
The Divinity School, Duke University, Durham, NC (New Testament)

MIROSLAV VOLF
Fuller Theological Seminary, Pasadena, CA (Theology)

STANLEY WALTERS
Rosedale Presbyterian Church, University of Toronto, Toronto, Ontario, CANADA (Old Testament)

DONALD WARDLAW
MCCormick Theological Seminary, Chicago, IL (Sermon)

ANN O'HARA GRAFF
Loyola University, Chicago, IL (Systematic Theology)

RESPONDENTS

ANNA CASE-WINTERS
McCormick Theological Seminary, Chicago, IL

STEPHEN HALL
North Park College, Chicago, IL

WALTER LIEFELD
Trinity Evangelical Divinity School, Deerfield, IL

VERONICA MENDEZ
Mundelein Seminary of the University of St. Mary of the Lake, Mundelein, IL

JOHN T. PAWLIKOWSKI
Catholic Theological Union, Chicago, IL

GRAYDON F. SNYDER
Chicago Theological Seminary, Chicago, IL

PAUL WADELL
Catholic Theological Union, Chicago, IL

NORTH PARK THEOLOGICAL SEMINARY

SYMPOSIUM ON THE THEOLOGICAL INTERPRETATION OF SCRIPTURE

OCTOBER 14-16, 1994

"THE CHURCH"

GUEST LIST

Philip J. Anderson
Britt Bergstrom
Jolene Bergstrom-Carlson
James R. Bergquist
Robert V. Bergquist
Jackson M. Blanchard
François Bovon*
Carl E. Braaten*
John S. Bray*
Anna Case-Winters*
Richard W. Carlson*
Gregory A. Clark
Michelle Clifton
Tom Collins
Inagrace Dietterich
James D. Erickson
Steven Evans
Linda M. Forbes
Patrick A. Genseal
Susan Gittip
Ann O'Hara Graff*
Dikran Y. Hadidian
Stephen Hall*
Kevin J. Haan
Richard B. Hays*
Everett Jackson
Karl Klockars
Paul E. Koptak
Walter Liefield*
Stacey Littlefield
Eugene Lowe
Janet Lundblad
Veronica Mendez*
Donald G. Miller
Arthur A.R. Nelson
F. Burton Nelson
Jim Nelson
Carol M. Noren
John T. Pawlikowski*
Francisco M. Ramos
Julie Shinn
Klyne R. Snodgrass*
Graydon F. Snyder*
Cathy Stanley
Norma Sutton
Johannes Van Der Ven
Judy Volf
Miroslav Volf*
Paul Wadell*
Stanley D. Walters*
Don M. Wardlaw*
C. John Weborg
Wayne Weld
Sigurd F. Westburg
Everett L. Wilson

* Program Participant

EX AUDITU
VOLUMES AVAILABLE

EX AUDITU Vol. 1 (1985) consists of selected articles presenting the issues inherent in the theological interpretation of Scripture.

EX AUDITU Vol. 2 (1986) discusses the theme: "Church and State Relationship." In addition there are two lead articles, one by Peter Stuhlmacher on "EX AUDITU and the Theological Interpretation of Holy Scripture," and the second by Ben F. Meyer on "The Primacy of Consent and the Uses of Suspicion."

EX AUDITU Vol. 3 (1987). The theme is: "Creation."

EX AUDITU Vol. 4 (1988). The theme is: "The Church and Israel (Romans 9-11)."

EX AUDITU Vol. 5 (1989). The theme is: "What is Salvation?"

EX AUDITU Vol. 6 (1990). The theme is: "Prophetic and/or Apocalyptic Eschatology."

EX AUDITU Vol. 7 (1991). The theme is: "Christology and Incarnation."

EX AUDITU Vol. 8 (1992). The theme is: "Worship."

EX AUDITU Vol. 9 (1993). The theme is: "Resurrection."

EX AUDITU Vol. 10 (1994). The theme is: "The Church."

Ten copies or more of one volume may be purchased for $10.00 per copy from Pickwick Publications.

To be published in April 1995:
EX AUDITU Vol. 11 (1995). The theme will be: "Biblical Law and Liberty"

Pickwick Publications, 4137 Timberlane Drive
Allison Park, PA 15101-2932